ANTIQUE FAKES AND REPRODUCTIONS

BOOKS BY RUTH WEBB LEE

EARLY AMERICAN PRESSED GLASS
Enlarged and Revised

HANDBOOK OF EARLY AMERICAN PRESSED GLASS PATTERNS

SANDWICH GLASS
Enlarged and Revised

SANDWICH GLASS HANDBOOK

VICTORIAN GLASS

VICTORIAN GLASS HANDBOOK

ANTIQUE FAKES AND REPRODUCTIONS
Enlarged and Revised

PRICE GUIDE TO PATTERN GLASS

A HISTORY OF VALENTINES

NINETEENTH-CENTURY ART GLASS

CURRENT VALUES OF ANTIQUE GLASS

LEE AND ROSE

AMERICAN GLASS CUP PLATES

REPRODUCTION OF DIAMOND-QUILTED STIEGEL TYPE BOTTLE,
MADE IN SOUTH JERSEY.

ANTIQUE FAKES & REPRODUCTIONS

Enlarged and Revised

By
RUTH WEBB LEE

LEE PUBLICATIONS
WELLESLEY HILLS · · MASSACHUSETTS

Enlarged and Revised

Copyright, 1938, 1950, by Ruth Webb Lee

ISBN 0-910872-07-4

ACKNOWLEDGMENTS

It has been a source of great comfort to note the genuine interest expressed by both dealers and collectors when they learned of my intention to undertake the publication of a book dealing with antique fakes and reproductions. They all keenly appreciated the gravity of the present situation and voiced their willingness to co-operate in every way possible.

A most valuable contribution to this book, which I am sure will be read with much profit by everyone interested in American silver, is the chapter on silver forgeries and fakes by Dr. John Marshall Phillips. In his position as curator of the famous Garvan Collections of Yale University, as well as director of the Gallery of Fine Arts, he has had an unusual opportunity to detect and study spurious items, for the finest silver pieces as well as the cleverest fakes for years were offered to the great collector, Francis P. Garvan.

To George S. McKearin are due my particular thanks for much important information about the fake flasks and bottles on the market. George McKearin is always most gracious in lending a helping hand, as were the late Edwin Lefèvre and Harry Hall White, when the first edition of this book was written in 1938. Edgar F. Hoffman and Dr. Charles Osgood, two of our great bottle specialists, also rendered valuable assistance.

Frank S. Schwarz spent considerable time in research work and generously supplied me with valuable data on paperweights, particularly South Jersey types, and lent me numerous specimens for illustrations.

Without the kindly aid given by Floyd H. Griffith of Pittsburgh, Pa., it would not have been possible for the readers to have such a complete and careful analysis of the pitfalls to be encountered in collecting iron mechanical banks, as is given in this book. He also furnished several of the photographs, which would be most difficult to procure had he not spent so many years in collecting and studying his specialty.

At the time the first edition was written, the four cup plate specialists, Albert C. Marble, George L. Tilden, James H. Rose, and L. W. Wheelock gave me the benefit of their experience with fakes, and lent me several they had purchased for comparison and study, to use for illustrations.

Mr. and Mrs. Benjamin B. Blakeney rendered substantial assistance in ways for which I have always been most grateful.

Of those who kindly assisted me by the loan of specimens or by helpful information in 1938, when the first edition of this book came out, I gratefully acknowledge my obligations to Mrs. Austin Chilson, J. O. Corner, Albert Force, Neil C. Gest, Mrs. Fern Gibson, Mrs. Emma Goldsmith, Mr. and Mrs. Hobart Hollis, B. H. Leffingwell, Mrs. Lucien Marioneaux, Mrs. Elsa Sampson, Norman Sherwood, and Arthur Sussel.

Perhaps my greatest obligation is to the rank and file of conscientious dealers and collectors who, by their determined efforts in the struggle against the inroads of fakes, have given me encouragement in that cause and in the writing of *Antique Fakes and Reproductions*. At considerable pains, detailed lists of reproductions and related data in circulation were made available to me. Much of this material might have escaped my attention, were it not for their kindness in keeping me advised. Of necessity, these gracious people must remain anonymous, since to reveal their identity would advertise the writer's sources and so place the unscrupulous on guard.

To combat the selling of spurious pieces, a number of dealers about the country have set up exhibits of fakes, in their shops. No more effective way to inspire confidence can be devised than to show customers the differences between the old and the new. George McKearin has a splendid permanent exhibit of reproductions in his shop at Hoosick Falls, N. Y. A number of the early blown fakes illustrated in this volume are from his collection.

As for the author, she has also collected fakes, one specimen of each, from the time that the new Turkey jam jar made its appearance in the 1920's. Some of these fakes are now valuable, since they were individual pieces produced by workmen who have since passed on. When the earliest pieces were acquired, it was never anticipated that the day would come when one might boast of owning one of the finest collections of counterfeits!

Ruth Webb Lee

CONTENTS

                                                              PAGE

ACKNOWLEDGMENTS vii

CHAPTER

I. PURPOSE 3

II. CONCERNING SOME REPRODUCTIONS 7

III. BLOWN GLASS 11

IV. HISTORICAL FLASKS 51

V. REPRODUCTION AND SOUVENIR CUP PLATES . . 75

VI. PATTERN GLASS REPRODUCTIONS 85

VII. MILK-WHITE GLASS 177

VIII. PAPERWEIGHTS 188

IX. LAMPS AND GLOBES 211

X. BOHEMIAN GLASS 227

XI. DOLPHIN CANDLESTICKS AND COMPOTES . . . 237

XII. FAKED AMERICAN SILVER 244

XIII. CERAMICS 253

XIV. MECHANICAL BANKS, OLD AND NEW 269

XV. IRONWORK 284

XVI. NOVELTIES 291

INDEX 305

xi

ILLUSTRATIONS

PLATE   PAGE

Reproduction of diamond-quilted Stiegel type bottle, made in
South Jersey . . . . *Frontispiece*

1 Examples of South Jersey reproductions in circulation between
1920 and 1925 15

2 South Jersey reproductions made in Clayton, N. J., about
1928–30, in varying shades of blue 16

3 South Jersey reproductions 17

4 Genuine early New York State milk bowl 18

5 South Jersey reproductions 19

6 South Jersey reproductions 20

7 South Jersey reproductions 24

8 Modern blown glass hats made in South Jersey 25

9 South Jersey reproductions 26

10 South Jersey reproductions 27

11 Reproduction South Jersey sugar bowl and miniature pieces . 28

12 South Jersey reproductions 29

13 Pair of South Jersey decanters and a hat 30

14 Modern South Jersey lily pad bowls, and a jug 31

15 Counterfeit lily pad pitcher, and blown three-mold bottle in
amethyst 34

16 Early group of fake blown three-mold glass 35

17 Copies of blown three-mold glass, produced in the 1930's . 35

18 Blown three-mold, produced in the 1930's 36

19 New blown three-mold hat, modern commemorative cup plate 37

20 Gift shop blown three-mold, made in many colors . . . 38

21 Czechoslovakian "Stiegel" which should deceive no one . . 42

22 Modern Mexican glass, including Virgin bottle 43

23 Modern Mexican glass 44

24 Modern Mexican glass 45

25 Air-twist, or "cotton-stem" glasses, made in New England . 46

26 Miniature blown glass creamers, Venetian and Bristol types.
Copies of early cotton-stem glasses 47

27 An import from Czechoslovakia 48

28 Fake Horse and Cart—"Success to the Railroad." Fake Plantation Bitters bottle 57

29 Fake Washington bottle, and Cornucopia-Basket of Fruit . . 58

30 Fake Fislerville Jenny Lind made in Czechoslovakia, and New
Washington "Calabash" bottle 59

xiii

PLATE   PAGE

31 South Jersey copy of Jenny Lind. Mexican bottle. Modern
    lacy plate   60
32 Old Log Cabin Booz bottle. Lowell Railroad-Eagle fake . .   61
33 Lowell-Railroad, Reverse, Washington   62
34 Czechoslovakian fake marketed years ago   67
35 Genuine Stiegel diamond-quilted bottle   68
36 Czechoslovakian bottle on left. On right, two South Jersey
    fakes   69
37 Modern South Jersey bottles   70
38 Modern South Jersey bottles   71
39 Four reproduction cup plates   76
40 Four reproduction cup plates   77
41 Three reproduction cup plates   78
42 Four modern souvenir plates   79
43 Two modern Washington souvenir cup plates. Open-edge
    dish not a true cup plate. Odd plate is old but has serrated
    edge ground off   80
44 Objects produced from new Horn of Plenty tumbler mold .   89
45 New Overlay tumbler. Daisy and Button Hand vase. Horn of
    Plenty tumbler   90
46 Star with Dewdrop seven-and-one-quarter-inch plate . . .   91
47 Reproduction Wildflower goblet is on the right   92
48 Reproduction Wildflower plate is on the right   93
49 Reproduction Westward-Ho goblet is on the right . . .   94
50 Westward-Ho lamp made from new goblet mold. Reproduc-
    tion Dolphin compote   95
51 Reproduction Rose in Snow goblet is on the right   98
52 Reproduction Rose in Snow plate is on the right   99
53 Moon and Star counterfeits   100
54 Reproduction Cherry, Daisy and Button, and Moon and Star
    goblets   101
55 Reproduction Ivy in Snow, New England Pineapple, and Fine
    Rib goblets   102
56 Hobnail vases on the market for the past twenty-five years .   107
57 Hobnail types never made in old glass   108
58 Hobnail reproductions on the market for years   109
59 Modern opal fruit goblet. Modern opalescent Hobnail goblet   110
60 Rose-opalescent Hobnail from Czechoslovakia   111
61 Hobnail reproductions   112
62 Old and new barber bottles. An original is on the left . .   113
63 New Hobnail sauce dish and salt. Novelty hat in case glass.
    Modern Thumbprint goblet   114
64 Novelty sugar and creamer simulating a pump and trough. The
    old are on the left   115
65 Modern forms in a Hobnail goblet, and Daisy and Button. In
    the center is a new "Lacy Sandwich"   119

PLATE   PAGE
66   Daisy and Button fakes. Copies of Hand vases   120
67   Daisy and Button plate and deep dessert dish. Two sizes in
        new Daisy and Button slippers, and a baby shoe in Marble
        glass   121
68   Modern plates in Spray and Cane, and Daisy and Button . .   122
69   Reproduction Daisy and Button goblets and champagnes. New
        Hand vase   123
70   Copy of early blown goblet. Fake Daisy and Button goblet .   124
71   Old and new Spanish Lace tumblers, and milk-white Black-
        berry goblets. The fakes are on the right   129
72   Lion pattern. The center piece is old—the sugar bowl and
        spoon holder are reproductions   130
73   Two new Lion celery vases   131
74   Old and new Lion sauce dish. The fake is on the right . .   132
75   The reproduction Lion goblet is on the right   133
76   Old and new Thousand Eye goblets. Reproduction Hobnail
        creamer, and a shoe   139
77   Old and new Shell and Tassel goblet. The copy is on the right   140
78   Reproduction Paneled Thistle, Cherry, and Pleat and Panel
        goblets   141
79   Reproduction Inverted Thumbprint tumbler and finger bowl.
        The old tumbler is in the center. Three Paneled Grape
        tumblers. The one in the center is old, the others new .   142
80   Enlarged detail in old and new Three Face goblets. The one
        on the left is old   143
81   Old and new Ribbon goblets. The fake is on the right. Three
        copies of cranberry Inverted Thumbprint   144
82   Reproduction and old Tulip wines, and Beaded Grape goblets.
        The fakes are on the right   145
83   Old and new Baltimore Pear goblet. The fake is on the right   146
84   Old and new Strawberry and Currant goblet. New Frosted
        Circle and Roman Rosette goblets   147
85   Old and new Crystal Wedding compotes. The reproduction is
        on the right   154
86   Old and new Ruby Thumbprint goblets, the original being on
        left. New shoe, and copy of Staffordshire vase, made in
        Portugal   155
87   All reproductions of colored Inverted Thumbprint, except the
        pitcher on the left   156
88   Modern goblets which are not copies of designs in early glass   157
89   Modern plate, not to be confused with any old one . . .   158
90   Modern plates, not related to any old ones   159
91   Original lacy Sandwich Beehive plate which has been repro-
        duced in many sizes and colors. New "Lacy Sandwich"
        plate. This design is copied in many forms   160
92   Reproductions of old style "Silvered" or Mercury glass . .   161

PLATE   PAGE

93   Curtain tiebacks, jam jars, pickle jars, and various objects as introduced over twenty-five years ago 162

94   New milk-white pieces 179

95   Modern milk-white Rabbit and Kitten plates 180

96   New Lace Dewdrop goblets. Modern Satin glass vase . . 181

97   Reproduction hen dish in purple Marble glass. Vallerysthal five-and-one-quarter-inch Swan covered dish 182

98   Three rare old paperweights. Those at end are dated Baccarat 193

99   Three choice old paperweights 194

100   Pieces used in genuine old paperweights 195

101   On the left, genuine Millville Rose. On the right, first attempt to copy it 196

102   Old Millville Rose at left, with two copies 197

103   Fake Mushroom paperweight on the left, old one on right. Modern paperweight perfume bottle in center 198

104   These new weights are more attractive than a photograph can show 203

105   Modern Chinese paperweights 204

106   American weight at top. Dated English weight in center. Chinese at bottom. All are new 205

107   Modern paperweights 206

108   Modern paperweights. The one at right has interlaced background 207

109   Modern paperweights 208

110   Modern "Three Pigs" and "Three Birds" paperweights . . 209

111   Lamps and wall sconces as presented twenty-five or more years ago 213

112   Reproductions of early Sandwich glass lamps 214

113   There are many styles of new Hurricane globes, as well as lamps and shades 215

114   Modern overlay colored lamps 216

115   Candlesticks. Sandwich style lamp. Overlay lamp . . . 217

116   Westward-Ho lamp converted from new goblet mold . . . 218

117   Reproduction of early Sandwich lamp in opaque jade-green and translucent white 219

118   Three designs in new girandoles 220

119   Girandoles and overlay lamp 221

120   New hanging lamps 222

121   New lamp globes 223

122   Array of Bohemian engraved pieces 229

123   Ruby Bohemian wine and liqueur sets, imported during past thirty years 230

124   Engraved ruby Bohemian glass. Note the two different styles of candlesticks 231

125   Finer engraved pieces, not seen so frequently as the table set in the center 232

PLATE   PAGE

126 Imported ruby Bohemian glass, which has been widely dis-
     tributed   233
127 Ruby Bohemian cordial and liqueur sets   234
128 Old and new dolphin candlesticks. The fake is on the right . 239
129 Old and new dolphin candlesticks. An original is on the right 240
130 Old and new dolphin compote. The fake is on the right . .   241
131 Teapot purporting to be by John Coney (1655–1722) . .   245
132 Base of teapot showing crude attempts at forging Coney's
     stamp   246
133 Genuine beaker made in 1685 by Cornelis Vanderburch . . 247
134 Dutch beaker, 1686, bearing a forged stamp of Vanderburch's 248
135 English beaker bearing a forged mark of John Burt's on the
     side   249
136 The base of the forged Burt beaker showing bruises where
     hallmarks have been erased   250
137 Three different pink luster tea sets in the House pattern . . 255
138 Gold and silver resist. Sunderland luster Liverpool jug . . 256
139 Modern copper luster   257
140 Wedgwood style porcelain imitations   258
141 Staffordshire animals and miniature tobies. Each one on the
     left is old   261
142 Staffordshire groups, all imported   262
143 Staffordshire figures, imported during the past thirty years . 263
144 Staffordshire reproductions   264
145 Staffordshire animals, all imported   265
146 New milk-white swan salt and a rooster paperweight from
     Czechoslovakia. Two fake Staffordshire animals . . .   266
147 Copies of beautiful overlay glass in colors. Dresden style toilet
     set and shoe   267
148 Trick Elephant. Jolly Nigger. Paddy and his Pig 271
149 Feed the Kitty. Cat Chases Mouse into Building   272
150 Two views of Presto savings bank   273
151 The Gem. Trick Dog. Tabby bank   274
152 Owl bank, original on left. Boy and Bull Dog. Darky on
     Bucking Mule   275
153 Bull Dog savings bank. Action ready to take coin. Rare
     original bank   276
154 Squirrel bank. Tricky Pig bank   277
155 Iron hitching post and garden accessories from Virginia . . 285
156 Reproductions of favorite patterns in old iron garden furniture 286
157 Iron urns and a garden table   287
158 Copies of foot-scrapers, early lanterns and other iron ware . 288
159 New fireplace fenders   289
160 An old and a new Victorian basket. An original is at the right 295
161 Modern hat, in an extra-large size   296
162 New English Hobnail hat. Modern Butterfly toddy plate . 297

PLATE   PAGE
163   Modern novelties. The bird salt at the end is old   298
164   Modern novelties. The second bird salt from the end is old .   299
165   Copy of an early Sandwich vase   300
166   Gift shop merchandise, not to be confused with old pieces.
         Paperweights which came out some years ago   301

Chapter 1

PURPOSE

A desire to meet the widespread demand from collectors and dealers in antiques for information that will help them to distinguish reproductions from originals is responsible for this book. An intelligent and patriotic interest in Americana has grown to such proportions that an extraordinary increase in the number of collectors and dealers throughout the country was inevitable. The rise in the demand necessarily led to a corresponding rise in prices and a high level of values in turn made fraud profitable. At all times, fakers have taken advantage of popular fads to foist imitations on eager but uninformed buyers. The greater the demand for a particular line of antiques, the more difficult it becomes to find genuine pieces, for the supply grows scantier. Always in a rising market the fake appears, never ostentatiously, never frankly labeled, until victimized buyers grow cautious. Once suspicions as to genuineness are aroused, the buying slows up and sometimes the demand is killed entirely. It was the prevalence of fakes that nearly put an end to the fad for early American pine furniture and interiors.

There is profit enough in selling authentic antiques at reasonable prices. Reputable dealers can afford to pay well for genuine pieces because they cater to a class of buyers who realize that rarity and historical association differentiate the antiques business from ordinary commercial lines.

Irrespective of differences of opinion as to artistic merit, workmanship, rarity, or historical association, it cannot be denied that more Americans today are collecting our early pattern glass than any other one line. It has been a commonplace of the antiques trade that throughout depression years the most active demand, North, South, East and West, has been for early American pressed glass. There are sound reasons why this should be the case. So rapid and extensive was the growth of interest in this glass that reproductions promptly made their appearance. Today there are so many reproductions and imitations on the market that both collectors and dealers are confronted by a situation so serious that something must be done soon to overcome it. No individual can do much. There must be concerted action by associations of dealers or collectors. It is my firm conviction that the glass clubs of this country have the opportunity to render a great service not only to their own members but to all collectors. The existing clubs should get together and organize a movement to check fraudulent practices. It will take collective effort to obtain legislative action. As this book goes to press, legislative action toward marking reproductions appears to be well under way.

There is nothing to be said against the manufacture of reproductions or copies of old originals by anyone. A cabinetmaker who copies a Chippendale chair and sells it as such operates a legitimate business. But if the dealer to whom he sells that chair in turn sells it as an original piece "of the period," he is clearly guilty of obtaining money under false pretenses. The harm is not in making or selling reproductions. It is the selling of reproductions at exorbitant prices and representing them to be authentic antiques. This constitutes fraud and is a menace to the layman as well as to the trade. By the same token, so is the sale of all reproductions of all antiques, whether glass, furniture, pottery or silver.

The permanent cure lies in education, furthered by a law against this particular form of misrepresentation. The ignorant collector who merely follows fads is apt to forget that there is no royal road to knowledge and that the phrase *caveat emptor* was coined a great many centuries ago. If he does not choose to protect himself by knowing what he buys, he will find an abundance of sellers whom he invites to fatten on his ignorance. A merely superficial acquaintance with what he collects may prove worse than utter ignorance. He may know enough about the market to realize that a Duncan Phyfe sofa or a Paul Revere tea service is very valuable. When fakes are offered to him at bargain prices, he swallows the hook as well as the bait, for it is difficult to resist an apparent bargain. He thinks that the dealer is an ignoramus and that he himself is so wise that by paying one dollar he in turn will get a ten-dollar bill.

I regret the necessity for expressing my conviction that the majority of the small and particularly the "amateur" dealers throughout the country also sadly need educating. Broadly speaking, dealers may be divided into three classes: The reputable and well informed, the ignorant, and the downright dishonest. If collectors exercised the discrimination when purchasing antiques that they do when they buy diamonds or when they select a family physician, there would be fewer complaints. The ignorant dealer is dangerous because he may, in good faith, sell as old what is really new. He is a victim of his ignorance when he cannot tell a reproduction from an original. He is easily deceived by clever, dishonest "pickers" and he often trades as well with dishonest dealers, victimizing his customers in the end without intending to do so. The unscrupulous dealer, of course, knows full well what he is doing when he preys on the ignorance or the greed of uninformed purchasers. Rare discrimination is ofttimes required in separating the wheat from the chaff.

I wish to stress again that only co-operation by clubs and societies of collectors may succeed in forcing the enactment of laws making it a crime to sell as antique that which is new. The reputable dealers also should immediately organize an association requiring its members not only to guarantee the genuineness of the antiques they sell but also to make good their guarantee. A membership card properly displayed should be a sign of responsibility. Violation of the code, when proven, would forfeit the membership.

A primary object of this book is to illustrate many of the reproductions now flooding the market and to point out the differences or variations between new and old. It is impossible to illustrate or even to list all the fakes that one may find today, for some were blown by individual workers for themselves or as gifts to friends and so were not widely distributed. It is fair to state here that the majority of the makers of reproductions do not misrepresent their products but sell them as reproductions at reproduction prices. Such pieces really belong in gift shops and department stores rather than in antique shops.

When the first edition of the author's *Early American Pressed Glass* came out in December, 1931, an enthusiastic collector from Philadelphia wrote: "Does the thought ever come to you that if the demand for this pressed glass keeps on increasing there will inevitably be reproductions on such a scale that it will kill off popular interest in it? What is the answer?"

The answer is that no racket should be allowed to kill a good legitimate business. It is necessary, instead, to kill the racket.

A "reproduction" becomes a "fake" only when it is sold as a genuine antique. The making of fakes is a very old story. It goes back thousands of years. Of course, there is no faking when there is no profit. It is too much to hope that any human agency can end all cheating. But the best way to cheat the cheaters lies in learning to tell the genuine from the imitation. This book is written in the hope that with its help buyers may find it easier to detect at least some of the frauds that are daily offered for sale to buyers of antiques. It is also well to bear in mind that knowledge will prevent excessive suspicion. Let the buyer beware of fakes but, also, let him beware of suspecting genuineness when there is really no basis for that suspicion. Dealers too often hear clients say that they will not buy this or that article because there are so many fakes. To stop collecting through the fear of being cheated is as foolish as to buy indiscriminately, and many a collector has missed getting fine pieces through unjustified skepticism.

Pick your dealer and let him guarantee that what he sells as old is really old and that your money will be cheerfully and promptly refunded if the goods are not as represented. It is as absurd to think that all dealers knowingly sell fakes as to assert that all lawyers are shysters or all physicians quacks.

Chapter II

CONCERNING SOME REPRODUCTIONS

When cultured Americans discovered over a generation ago, that they did not have to buy all their antiques in European shops and palaces, and that it was more patriotic and more satisfying to "buy American," collectors multiplied. They no longer had to cross the ocean to find treasures about which they could boast more proudly. One line became popular, then another, until early American glass came into its own. At first every piece was Stiegel or Wistarberg, naturally enough since the craving for labels is merely the commercial need of "attributions" to make a piece more costly. Much Bristol, old but not Stiegel, was attributed to the Baron and cost ten times as much as it did in England where it remained merely Bristol. Wistarberg was sought for the same reason and much Nailsea is still labeled Wistarberg in famous collections. Then came the craze for cruder forms of early American blown glass and "South Jersey" and "New York State" and "New England" glass soared in price. Reproductions and fakes began to make their appearance the moment it paid to make them, though never in great quantities.

Collectors of the most popular of all early American lines of glass are now advised to beware of pattern glass because there are so many reproductions on the market—as though the same thing could not be said of all antiques! There is not a day that I do not receive from six to twenty letters asking whether it is safe to collect this or that particular pattern because the writers have been assured that reproductions are sold as old in shops. Collectors report that dealers who have stocks of blown glass often tell inquirers that they will not handle pressed glass because it is all being faked. And when the same customers go to a dealer who happens to specialize on pattern glass, they are apt to hear that anything which is not in stock in the shop is absent because it is being reproduced

7

and, of course, he does not handle undesirable pieces. Collectors too often are frightened out of completing sets because of such false rumors. It is time lovers of early American glass were apprised of the facts, for their own piece of mind as well as for the good of the trade.

The first real alarm among pattern glass collectors was felt about sixteen years ago, when the Horn of Plenty water tumbler made its appearance. Having been an enthusiastic collector of that pattern myself for many years, I immediately felt that probably every other item would follow and the value of my set be ruined. The set included nearly every rarity. I disposed of it and it has been one of my greatest regrets that I did so. Being of lead-flint glass, it was not easy to reproduce skillfully enough to deceive experienced collectors. The water tumbler, new or old, lacks the clear bell tone when tapped that will come from almost any other genuine old piece, due to the thickness and shape and to the heavy base; but while the old tumblers ring a little and the new not at all, the resonance is not the reliable test here as it is of other forms. In old pieces there is a softness of contours, however, that is absent in the new. For example, the diamond points in the genuine Horn of Plenty design are softly rounded, while on the new they are outstandingly sharp and pointed. The old ones had a ground-out pontil mark on the base which left the rim of the ground-out space sharp and uneven. This effect is reproduced on the new glasses but it is smooth, because the rounded space is merely pressed instead of being cut out by a grinding wheel. It is much simpler to reproduce the later patterns because they were made of lime glass, which came into general use after the Civil War. Lime was a profitable substitute for the more expensive lead-flint which gave the older glass the weight and the clear resonance of tone when tapped that every collector loves to hear.

The next imitation was the ever-popular overlay lamp. Most collectors are familiar with the beautiful two-toned effects in lamp bowls, such as amethyst cut through to clear, opaque-white to jade-green, etc. The same importing house which brought over the Horn of Plenty tumblers also flooded the market with pear-shaped lamp bowls in various color combinations. Whether the importers foresaw it or not, one result was to arouse the cupidity of unscrupulous dealers. An ingenious rascal saw still greater profit by "improving" the goods. He bought every old marble-base lamp which he could obtain cheaply, chiefly those having a plain, clear glass bowl. Old milk-white bases also were used. The plain and unattractive bowl was removed, and the beautiful new reproduction reset with the aid of plaster of Paris. These were then dirtied up, wrapped in old newspapers and peddled from shop to shop and from city to city. Dealers eagerly purchased fine-looking overlay lamps, with bases that were obviously old, at anywhere from $12.00 to $18.00, for which collectors would pay from $25.00 to $50.00 fifteen years ago. The credulous dealer doubled his money. The faker more than quadrupled his.

When I begged one trade magazine to expose these fakers at the time, I was told that it was only greed on the part of the dealers who bought them that was responsible for the fraud and that they eventually would get what was coming to them. It was neither a fair nor an intelligent attitude for a trade magazine to take, since its livelihood came from the advertisements of honest dealers and from subscribers who were entitled to the protection afforded by the exposure of frauds. Its obvious duty was to warn honest but unwary dealers.

Complete lamps were also manufactured and sold but these were more easily detected than when the old base was combined with the new bowl. The collar of the new lamps exposed the fraud. On the old, the collars were chiefly of brass and sometimes of pewter. On the new, they were obviously not old. To be sure, the new collars could be removed and replaced by old, but the telltale fresh plaster of Paris always showed where they were cemented on. Another giveaway was in the marble bases, when these were used. They were bound to look new. On Plate 111 are shown the types of overlay lamps which were first offered for sale as far back as twenty-five years ago. They are still being made in a number of patterns. Plates 114 and 115 display the newer styles that soon followed, and some of these are still on sale.

About eighteen years ago the same company produced and sold sconces with mirror reflectors (Plate 111) but these were too new looking to deceive anyone. Expert copies of sconces did come on the market later, some of which would challenge an expert to decide whether or not they were old. The plain, paneled type was more easily copied. The folded edges of the old ones were always rolled over a plain wire in order to keep them straight while the new ones were merely folded over and pressed down.

Among other fakes described in subsequent chapters are blown glass, pattern glass, Bohemian glass, dolphin candlesticks, cup plates, historical flasks, paperweights and silver, as well as various other lines.

Chapter III

BLOWN GLASS

Much territory must be covered today in dealing with reproductions of our old blown glass, for not only have they been made by American workers, since the demand from collectors meant high prices, but they have come from other countries in large quantities. For a number of years Bohemia, later Czechoslovakia, and Mexico led the procession of imports. Again the harm does not lie in selling reproductions but in selling new-glass as old at old-glass prices, as some unscrupulous dealers are doing.

Curiously enough, most of the copies of our early blown glass have been made in South Jersey, near the spot from which many of the originals came. They have been produced, sometimes by groups, and again by individuals. These will be described here, in the order of their appearance.

The earliest known blown glass reproductions of which I can find any record were made by a group of experienced glass blowers familiar with the Jersey technique, in South Jersey, from about 1920 to 1925. Apparently the venture did not prove profitable because nothing more was heard from them after this short period. Plate 1 illustrates four examples of the work done by this particular group.

Following closely on the heels of the first South Jersey reproductions, there began to appear along about 1930, such individual pieces as those illustrated on Plates 2 and 3. The examples on Plate 2 are particularly interesting in view of the indifferent and careless workmanship displayed in pieces turned out a few years later. These early reproductions were produced in Clayton, N. J., in varying shades of dark blue, as well as in amber, and a shade of green deeper than aquamarine. In studying the pieces illustrated, it will be noted that they have character, and that they are ruggedly individualistic. The amber bowl, hourglass and wine glass on

11

Plate 3 undoubtedly belong to the same group but were not made in quantity. While it is possible to detect these frauds by various means, such as weight (reproductions are invariably much heavier) texture, workmanship and usual signs of age, we must bear in mind that excellent individual pieces were made from time to time, the extent of which it is impossible to enumerate since they were often blown after hours as gifts to friends and relatives. This is a practice which was carried on in glass factories for a great many years. Since the workmen followed the old methods and techniques up until the present era, even experts cannot always fix the age of some items within perhaps thirty years. This holds true of any good South Jersey pieces.

The lamps and turtle doorstops shown on Plate 3 were apparently first marketed some time between 1928 and 1930. They were continued over a period of years. The lamps were sold by the barrelful to any number of antique dealers. Turtle doorstops in many solid colors were seen frequently in shop windows in such places as Atlantic City and throughout the "antiques" section of Philadelphia.

Apparently another group of South Jersey glass blowers began operations during the early 1930's, in the Millville-Vineland section of Jersey. Along about 1933, I was taken to see a veritable warehouse full of new blown glass, in this area. I acquired for comparison and study quite a quantity of these reproductions. Some of it I still own. The balance I gave to an interior decorator for use in her business as interesting examples of modern blown glass made in the old-fashioned way. She sold them for exactly what any department store would have charged. Some of these pieces I am using here for the same purpose for which I bought them; that is, for comparison with the old. At the time they were purchased I did not foresee that the day would come when I would avail myself of them for illustrations in a book written to warn the unwary.

I am convinced that the South Jersey man who first planned to market these blown glass reproductions on a commercial scale did not intend to injure anyone. In fact, his circulars read:

These reproductions of early South Jersey hand-blown glass are made by hands which made glass forty or fifty years ago; products which are now prizes for the lucky collector who can buy them. These reproductions are made adjoining the site where great factories stood for decades and are faithful and true to the old traditions in size, color and style—the Jersey glass which commands a high premium today.

When these skillful men, the last of their type, pass on with the art and the secrets handed down to them by their forbears, the same glass will increase in value from year to year. Many old pieces of these very types have been sold to museums and private collectors for big prices.

These workmen took pride in what they did. The main trouble with the new South Jersey glass was that a good deal of it was not annealed properly and it cracked and broke much more readily than the average old pieces. I know of shipments containing both old pieces and new reproductions that arrived at their destination with several new pieces cracked by the cold but all of the old intact. A Pennsylvania dealer told me that for many years one of his tests for South Jersey glass consisted of pouring cold water into the pitchers. The old ones stood it and the reproductions did not.

It was the output of this particular South Jersey group that first started the agitation about glass fakes—an agitation that never went much further than a few more or less futile discussions at glass club meetings at which a limited number of pieces were on exhibition. The main trouble, of course, can be traced directly to those unscrupulous dealers who bought this glass as new and sold it for old. The trade today faces a serious crisis unless this practice is stopped and stopped without delay. That is why I stress again and again the vital need of thoroughly educating both dealers and collectors, since recourse to law is likely to be slow, expensive and uncertain under existing conditions.

From this Millville-Vineland section came copies of the large blown early so-called "milk bowls," in amber, aquamarine, and sapphire blue. These appeared about 1933. An excellent example of an old bowl similar to those copied, is shown on Plate 4. The old ones have a decided ring to the glass when tapped which the new ones lack entirely, so it is a critical test for bowls, so long as the quality of the new glass remains as it always has been. Good copies of creamers with applied handles were produced in various sizes, and in the same colors as the bowls. They also lack the bell tone of the old. One of the creamer reproductions of this period is pictured on Plate 5.

The line of new copies of offhand blown South Jersey pieces, such as I saw and purchased in 1933, is shown on Plates 5 and 6. There were pitchers, large and small; vases, finger bowls, tall glasses, dessert dishes with a folded rim, and another style not pictured, which was flaring, and with a crimped foot. Other products included beer sets of a style never found among genuine antiques —a pitcher, and mugs in deep blue, emerald green, and amber; bulbous-shaped vases in fine shades of color, with and without decorative applied handles. There were witch balls in many colors. Decorators found the latter useful for spots of color. They also made the reproductions of the famous Booz Log Cabin bottle shown on Plate 32. Plain blown hats were made in different sizes and colors, and many of them were excellent copies. So many of the early hats, particularly the heavy Ohio types, did not carry any resonance when tapped that this favorite test fails on such pieces. The reproduction hats really did harm, for there is no sure way to identify them from the old, except possibly by the use of the ultraviolet rays now employed when the investment justifies the trouble. A collector of hats who does not have enough experience to judge accurately should call on an expert, or else resign himself to the hazards of buying spurious items occasionally. As a matter of fact, some of these early copies of hats are rare today.

The foregoing covers nearly all the reproductions turned out by one of the most prolific group of makers of the earlier so-called "South Jersey" fakes—incidentally a line that has been discontinued for some time. In passing, it may be noted that such pieces, actually reproductions of early glass, were all of plain early primitive types, rather than styles so often associated with "South Jersey," decorated with lily pads and applied threads. The output

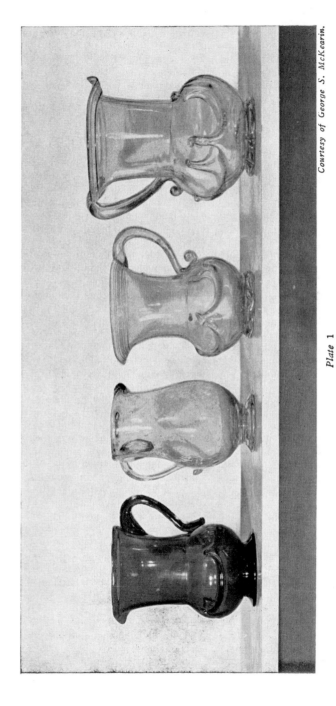

Plate 1   *Courtesy of George S. McKearin.*

EXAMPLES OF SOUTH JERSEY REPRODUCTIONS IN CIRCULATION BETWEEN 1920 AND 1925.

Cobalt blue lily-pad pitcher; plain pale aquamarine pitcher, streaked with green. Two lily-pad pitchers, in aquamarine, one with a decided yellow tone.

Plate 2

SOUTH JERSEY REPRODUCTIONS MADE IN CLAYTON, N. J., ABOUT 1928–30, IN VARYING SHADES OF BLUE.

At the same time, similar pieces were made in amber and an unusual shade of green, slightly darker than aquamarine.
Note the difference between these pieces and those of a slightly later date, shown on Plates 4 and 6.

Plate 3

SOUTH JERSEY REPRODUCTIONS.

The two South Jersey lamps, period 1928–30, are of particular interest since many have been sold in antique shops. Generally the bowls are colored and the stems clear. The large bowl in the center is amber. Later types were like that shown on Plate 4. Turtle doorstops were produced in many colors. The wine glass and hourglass are individual pieces, never made in quantity.

Plate 4

GENUINE EARLY NEW YORK STATE MILK BOWL.

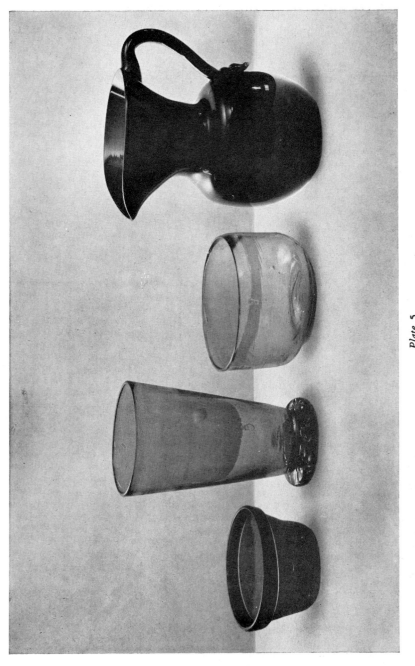

Plate 5

SOUTH JERSEY REPRODUCTIONS.

Plate 6

SOUTH JERSEY REPRODUCTIONS.

was all heavy, crude, and as stated before, so badly annealed that it cracked and broke easily. Only the most inexperienced collector could be deceived by it.

While visiting the Millville-Vineland section of New Jersey again in 1937–38, I discovered a new individual engaged in producing reproductions in wholesale lots. His types varied entirely from those made by the group of workmen during the earlier part of the 1930's. The maker was a foreigner who had a genuine love for his art. He showed me some of his products, including pieces resembling the Tiffany Favrile ware (now discontinued by that firm) which were quite artistic.

From the standpoint of art work, his glass was choice. Those which may be classed as "fakes" were interesting and some were beautiful in color, but they would not deceive an expert or even anyone who had studied old glass for any length of time. It was not revealed how the change in the character of his commercial output came about. From individual specimens of high-class work, he turned to blue, amethyst, and green imitations of Stiegel and Ohio Stiegel type bottles. These cannot be called exact copies of early American specimens. In his possession was one bottle mold which he claimed to be English and about seventy-five years old at that time. The bottles are fully dealt with and illustrated in the chapter devoted to historical flasks and bottles.

This individual workman's South Jersey reproductions at the time I saw them in 1938 consisted of diamond-quilted bottles in all sizes, from miniatures to full pints in amethyst, sapphire blue, and other colors. Plate 7. Hats were made to match many of the bottle patterns, including the diamond-quilted; heavy swirl; and a vertical rib in a broken bar effect. The rims were folded over properly and there were creditable pontil marks on the bases. But heft any of these hats and study the quality of the glass! They are all much too heavy and the glass poor in quality, giving forth no more sound when tapped than a dull thud. These tests always tell the story in hats of this type. Plate 8.

Other items from this particular maker included blown salts in a swirled pattern, caster bottles, creamers in various sizes and styles; sugar bowls both open and covered displaying the familiar South Jersey technique of threading and superimposing glass in the so-called lily pad effect; diamond-quilted and fluted sugar bowls in patterns matching the bottles, and miniature glass animals, bottles and creamers. See Plates 7, 9, 10, 11 and 12.

The first specimens of diamond-patterned sugar bowls and bottles could not be identified with the familiar "South Jersey" glass. The forms, color, and technique were different, but later the maker broadened the scope of his production and old-style threaded and lily pad pieces duly made their appearance.

The classification of South Jersey reproductions today must include all these lines. As with most individual glassworkers, skillful though they may be, he was not well informed on American antique forms, fortunately for collectors. Glass blowers often assert that they can reproduce any old glass closely enough to fool any expert, but so far I have never seen a reproduction in blown glass that could not be distinguished from the old when placed side by side, by anyone with years of practical experience plus a natural flair for glass. "Book knowledge" in itself is not enough. Many dealers in antiques today are afraid to buy, from time to time, fearing the pieces might turn out to be new fakes. Some collectors are beginning to view everything in shops with open suspicion. In fact, a few of them forget their manners and become downright insulting in their skepticism. Again I venture to suggest to such collectors that they take pains to acquire more knowledge instead of accusing all dealers of dishonesty or ignorance or both. At the same time, it must be admitted that a collector is justified in his suspicious attitude after he has been inveigled several times by different dealers into paying top prices for what turned out to be comparatively worthless new glass.

A few years after I visited the workshop of the glass blower whose wares have just been described, a friend called on me one day and displayed her latest acquisition, a pair of amethyst blown quart decanters with matching stoppers, in an expanded diamond-quilted pattern. No similar old ones are known to exist. They are illustrated on Plate 13. She paid $25.00 for them. A most painful duty when asked to express a candid opinion, is to have to enlighten credulous buyers. These decanters displayed every indication of being a more recent example from the hands of the same glass blower who produced the diamond-quilted "Stiegel" toilet bottles, hats, vases, and the like. While he worked in a number of colors, amethyst headed the list. The "rare color" tradition dies a hard death! These wares misled many unwary buyers, both dealers and collectors, until they became thoroughly known. Many are beautiful in color, but they are unlike the wares which were made in the early days in quality and workmanship.

The originals which he meant to reproduce are exquisite in texture and light in weight. The diamond-quilting is expanded more delicately without the thick lines which will be noted in the new. Fortunately for us, the maker often preferred to depend on his ingenuity to originate new forms instead of following the more difficult task of closely imitating the originals. Neither do any known examples exist of old hats or vases in a blown expanded diamond pattern to correspond with those which came on the market during the 1930's. Even when the worker knows his trade thoroughly, he finds it difficult, if not impossible, to control color; and so the cost of a really fine reproduction would be prohibitive. The disproportionate number of failures, in seeking to obtain the exact shade wanted, involves too great an expense. Moreover, there are not enough educated collectors of fine early blown glass tableware and bottles today to absorb a volume production at high prices.

Not long after the appearance of the quart amethyst decanters more South Jersey bowls came to light from an unknown source, usually adorned with threads and a heavy superimposed decoration of glass, known as lily pads. Two are pictured on Plate 14, showing a side view and one of the foot. These vary in size, measuring from nine inches to nine and three-quarter inches in diameter and three and one-quarter inches to four and one-half inches high. The color range was astonishing—brilliant dark emerald green, vivid sapphire blue, and bright purples. There were no true-to-color types. Neither the shapes nor the shades of color were right, nor

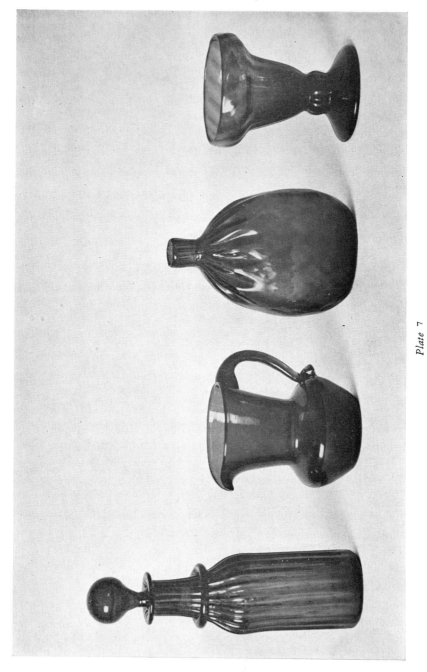

Plate 7

SOUTH JERSEY REPRODUCTIONS.

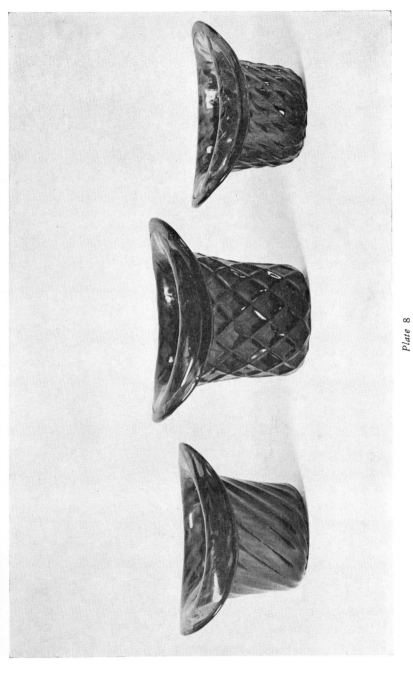

Plate 8

MODERN BLOWN GLASS HATS MADE IN SOUTH JERSEY.

Plate 9

SOUTH JERSEY REPRODUCTIONS.

Plate 10

SOUTH JERSEY REPRODUCTIONS.

Plate 11

REPRODUCTION SOUTH JERSEY SUGAR BOWL AND MINIATURE PIECES.

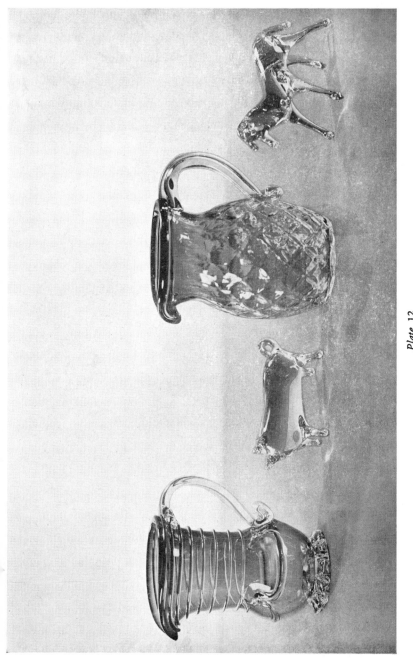

Plate 12

SOUTH JERSEY REPRODUCTIONS.

Plate 13
PAIR OF SOUTH JERSEY DECANTERS AND A HAT,
UNLIKE ANY OLD ONES.

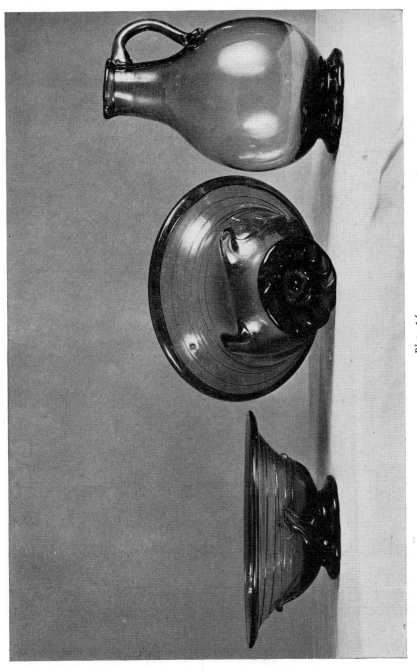

Plate 14

MODERN SOUTH JERSEY LILY-PAD BOWLS, AND A JUG.

the quality of the glass. The threads were added in such a careless manner that they often were allowed to run over the tips of the lily pad decoration. They were spread far apart and much too unevenly to deceive even inexperienced buyers. It is fair to state that these were not sold as old; but unfortunately we may be sure that many of them will eventually be offered as genuine to gullible buyers. History invariably repeats itself in the counterfeiting industry.

All old glass does not necessarily ring. For a time, dealers and collectors considered it a reliable test, but it is not always such. These new bowls do not ring, though most old ones do. The applied lily pad decoration is thicker than it should be, and is carelessly applied. Old pieces are lighter in weight, and the texture of the glass is different. "Texture" is difficult to describe, for words cannot convey it accurately. The surface of the old seems softer, not so harsh and brilliant looking. The bases on the old have acquired a soft worn appearance, quite different from the newly applied file scratches or emery cloth marks resorted to in order to simulate years of usage. While some early small pieces of glass may be old and still not show wear on the bases, large bowls are heavier and so should have natural wear.

Along with the lily pad bowls, there appeared many new styles of jugs and containers, with and without handles, in aquamarine and amber, as well as in other brighter colors. One such style is shown on Plate 14. One cannot expect to hear the old ring when one taps a flask or jug, though the other marks intended to suggest age, as described for the bowls, would apply to the bottles.

Pictured on Plate 15 is a brownish-purple pint pitcher which would certainly fool many people, unless they were extremely cautious. In many respects, it is the best reproduction of a lily pad piece I have seen. About the neck are quite convincing threads and the foot has been lightly but carefully crimped. The base displays the sort of wear that is usually seen on fakes; the scratches being easily distinguished by experts from the genuine evidence of the wear resulting from years of usage. The applied lily pad decoration is not so overdone as was the case with the new bowls.

In fact, the lily pads are not quite as distinct as they should be but the pitcher is without the frankly commercial aspects of the bowls. The pitcher was put out with the addition of wear marks to indicate age; therefore there was the intent to deceive. The handle might have been added in a more convincing way. The old ones almost invariably tapered with a delicate crimping, but this one was sheared off, leaving it flat and uneven. Even so, the chief points of difference between this pitcher and an old one are the quality and weight of the glass. It is *much* too heavy. A similar old pitcher would be much lighter; the base would not show such a great amount of wear; and, when tapped with a hard object, such as a pen or pencil, would not give off the dull, metallic clink heard from this one.

Some years ago a number of new blown diamond-quilted salts were made in New England, similar in shape to the salt on Plate 7. These were not only poor copies, but there was the usual dull thud to be expected from new glass when tapped. Creamers and other pieces were made at the same time, though not in large enough quantities to be very harmful. The fraud was exposed before they could be widely distributed, but the chief promoter more than broke even. While the resonance was lacking, the colors of the creamers were quite good.

A New York house imported and sold fifteen or twenty years ago a number of pieces in what has long been a favorite with collectors—blown three-mold. I refer to the blown glass known generically by that name and not to the pressed glass that shows three mold marks. At first, the line consisted of only five pieces; a covered sugar bowl, creamer, footed salt, sauce dish and a hat, all in clear glass, in the Sunburst pattern. The design was thin and not a careful copy of the old and the impressions were poor. The hats sold well, as I have seen them in antique shops in various sections of the country, but especially in the suburbs of Washington, D. C., on Pine Street in Philadelphia and Charles Street in Boston. Apparently the other pieces did not have a wide distribution. They were peddled chiefly by "pickers" or "runners" who sold them to small dealers at a moderate commercial profit. Plates 16 and 17.

The surest way to kill the reproduction racket is to have collectors find too many really rare pieces too often. When a piece which normally is seldom met with on collecting trips suddenly bobs up at every small shop, suspicion is inevitably aroused. But the maker has to sell in volume to pay for his trouble, hence the necessity of mass production in fakes. Inexpert collectors would not be too alert when asked to pay $4.00 or $5.00 for a blown three-mold hat that when genuine sold for $10.00 or $15.00. But when it came to the blown three-mold sugar bowls, rare enough to fetch high prices, the situation changed because the only buyers were apt to be persons who had a better knowledge of the genuine

Plate 15
COUNTERFEIT LILY-PAD PITCHER, AND BLOWN THREE-MOLD
BOTTLE IN AMETHYST.

Plate 16

EARLY GROUP OF FAKE BLOWN THREE-MOLD GLASS.

Plate 17

COPIES OF BLOWN THREE-MOLD GLASS, ORIGINALLY TERMED
"BLOWN MOLDED," PRODUCED IN THE 1930's, OR POSSIBLY EARLIER.

Plate 18

BLOWN THREE-MOLD PRODUCED IN THE 1930's.

NEW BLOWN THREE-MOLD HAT.

Plate 19

MODERN COMMEMORATIVE CUP PLATE.

Plate 20

GIFT SHOP BLOWN THREE-MOLD. MADE IN MANY COLORS.

article. The extremely poor workmanship combined with the "bargain price," instantly aroused suspicion instead of stimulating eagerness to buy.

The importing house that handled the blown three-mold line later changed to different models, some of which may be seen on Plate 18. The impressions are sharper. Happily enough, in some pieces they were much too sharp. Palpably brand-new molds replaced the old, to make the goods less easy to detect. But the latest pieces are no more right than the first ones were. It is desirable to include in any collection a few new pieces for comparison with the old. Buyers should know all the "Don'ts" as well.

The list of new blown three-mold items on the market in the latest versions include a "nut dish or ash tray" (sauce dish) three and one-half inches in diameter in the diagonal ribbing with sunburst. In fact, many of the pieces are still in the Sunburst pattern. Footed salts may be had in crystal, amber, or cobalt blue in two styles. The sugar bowl is made only in crystal and blue, but I daresay it might have been had in any color on order. Creamers come with or without a foot, the footed ones having been made in cobalt blue as well as in crystal. The colored pieces fooled a number of unwary buyers. Then there are wine glasses five and one-half inches in height, as well as water tumblers three and three-quarters inches high.

Before the new reproductions came on the market, only a few of the late Mr. Roosevelt's "economic royalists" could possibly afford to set their tables with blown three-mold glass. Today, even a poor Democrat may do it. The goblets wholesale at $7.20 per dozen. The hats, which, when genuine, sell readily in crystal at $10.00 to $15.00, may be had for fifty cents each.

All genuine blown three-mold glass should have a clear bell tone to the glass, so if you cannot tell an old piece from a new one in any other way, tap it. Also, some of the new shapes are unlike any known old ones. For example, there never was an old goblet made like the one illustrated, as far as is known. I know of but one lucky collector who owns a full-sized three-mold goblet and the design is different. This goblet has been thought to be foreign. There are two patterns of the fake. The salts do not bear dangerous resemblance to the old ones. The shape is not right. The foot is not right. The design is not right. There never was an old blown three-mold hat with a base like the new one shown on Plate 19. These may be encountered in a wide variety of colors. As reproductions, they were very poor, though a collector who did not know that such fakes were in circulation might casually pick up one of the hats at some small shop and not detect the fraud until he came to examine it critically.

When this ware was made originally in the first half of the nineteenth century it was blown into two-, three-, four- or five-part hinged molds and sometimes more. Except in some early Sandwich pieces, which were thick, such as inkwells and some of the crudest hats, the inside of the glass follows in ridges and hollows the patterns of the outside. By rubbing the fingers on the inside, one may feel these depressions. In most of the new ones, the inside is smooth, though in some of the latest line there are spots that are not smooth. Nevertheless, it is to be doubted whether it will ever pay fakers to copy both the perfections and the imperfections which, to an expert, clearly differentiate old "three-mold" from the new. There will always be something that does not click. No two old pieces are exactly alike, being individually made and, therefore, more expensive to manufacture at today's labor costs. Mass production will not do. It has been tried, though. Plate 20 pictures the latest copies. These particular pieces were purchased by the writer in New York City at Lord & Taylor's, about 1945. Pitchers, vases and decanters were all apparently produced from the quart decanter molds. These pieces were made in blue, emerald green, and in amethyst. If there are other colors, I have not seen them. They have been sold as new in the department stores and gift shops. Whether any of these pieces have wandered into antique shops so far, I cannot tell. There is nothing deceptive about the decanters or pitchers to the critical or informed buyer. The vase is not a copy of any known original.

One type of new glass that should not delude the merest amateur, is the Czechoslovakian "green, bubbly Stiegel glass" as it was once called. Dealers in modern glassware have displayed this line off and on for at least twenty-five years. It was for years regularly "planted" in Christian farm houses by unChristianlike "pickers" who swapped it with the farmers' wives for old pattern glass. It is decorative enough for some purposes, but it certainly has no legitimate place in antique shops or collectors' cabinets. The country was flooded with flip glasses, bowls, all sorts of wines and stemware; vases, pitchers, etc. A group of typical pieces is pictured on Plate 21.

From Czechoslovakia to Mexico is no distance at all, where such wares are marketed. Mexican blown glass is quite different from the other types described in this chapter, and yet many collectors and dealers have been confused by some of it. To begin with it is all of an inferior metal, full of small bubbles, and the pieces as a rule show a swirled or ribbed effect through the glass. In some articles, such as dessert dishes, pitchers, and vases, the rims are folded over in the old style, but the handles are practically never applied as they should be if they were American and of the period. None of the glass has any ring, cracking easily, as do many of the South Jersey reproductions, for the same reason—improper annealing.

The Madonna or Virgin bottles may be seen in department stores and gift shops and occasionally, I regret to say, in antique shops. They are found in many vivid colors. The modern Mexican glass is decorative enough, and doubtless many people find it useful, but it does not belong in antique shops. Representative groups may be seen on Plates 22, 23 and 24.

About twenty-five years ago, the Pairpoint Glass Company, at New Bedford, Mass., made quite an assortment of stemware after the style of many English glasses, sometimes referred to as "cotton stem" in this country. Two of this sort are shown on Plate 25. Most of the authentic glasses were so expertly made that they appeared to be all in one piece. In the new ones, the bowls are fused into the stem too clumsily to escape notice. The bases exhibit none of the distinguishing characteristics of the old ware, and are flat, instead of being cupped or domed, as they should be. Better copies

Plate 21

CZECHOSLOVAKIAN "STIEGEL" WHICH SHOULD DECEIVE NO ONE.

Plate 22
MODERN MEXICAN GLASS, INCLUDING VIRGIN BOTTLE.

Plate 23
MODERN MEXICAN GLASS.

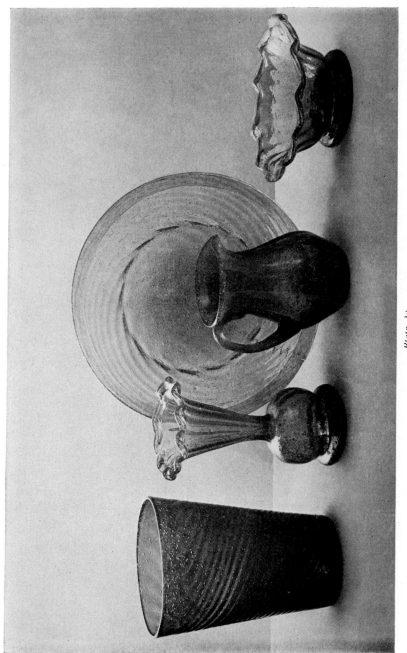

Plate 24

MODERN MEXICAN GLASS.

Plate 25
AIR-TWIST, OR "COTTON-STEM" GLASSES, MADE IN NEW ENGLAND.

MINIATURE BLOWN GLASS CREAMERS, VENETIAN AND BRISTOL TYPES.

Plate 26
COPIES OF EARLY COTTON-STEM GLASSES.

Plate 27
AN IMPORT FROM CZECHOSLOVAKIA.

are shown on Plate 26. These were imported from Czechoslovakia a number of years ago. They, too, lack the quality of the old.

A really attractive piece of modern Czechoslovakian glass is the vase shown on Plate 27. While this suggests the fine old Amelung glass which was made in Frederickstown, Md., after 1797, still it lacks several of the Amelung characteristics. I first found one in a gift shop in central New York, where both old and new glass was sold but nothing was misrepresented. There is no harm in buying or selling reproductions as such. Many families who cannot afford the antique-priced old, may enjoy the general effect of copies without depleting the pocketbook.

An importing house has recently sold to gift shops and department stores a large number of tiny miniature objects, made after the manner of some early Bristol and Venetian glass. Because some of these may ultimately find their way into antique shops, I am showing a group on Plate 26. These are obtainable in sapphire blue and various color combinations.

Before closing this discussion of that glass once termed "Blown Molded," but known today under the generic title of "blown three-mold," it seems in order to warn the reader that the cleverest forgeries evidenced in blown glass have appeared in this type. It is extremely unfortunate that not a specimen is available for illustration, for the frauds have been marketed with such circumspection that it is presently impossible to obtain a single item.

During the early 1930's, word reached the writer that some particularly fine reproductions of colored three-mold were offered to a prominent New York dealer, in most unusual shades. He did not purchase any. No more reports were heard and, after several years passed, these reproductions were forgotten. Then one day I attended a large auction sale and was seated next to an eminent collector whom I knew to be a keen student of early blown glass. As a beautiful three-mold dish in a peculiar shade of color was put up, he whispered, "This piece was offered to me by a Jersey dealer a number of years ago,* along with two other forms, at $50.00. I made a note of them and now here is the largest piece." It sold at

* I think 1933.

a high figure, after spirited bidding on the part of several dealers and collectors. Since that time, I have heard of several other pieces which apparently belong to this same group.

As nearly as the picture can be pieced together, these particular fakes are characterized by off-shades of color unusual in blown three-mold, fine workmanship, a certain amount of ring to the glass and they are sufficiently well simulated to pass some experts —but not all of them. It would appear that a highly skilled workman had spent considerable time and very likely considerable expense, in producing the nearly perfect fake. The gamble has seemed to pay off though it seems doubtful if it will in the long run.

Chapter IV

HISTORICAL FLASKS

Collectors of historical flasks so far have had no more occasion to worry over fakes than collectors of cup plates. There have been too few to cause real trouble. The reason probably is that there are fewer buyers of flasks and cup plates than of pattern glass. To be profitable, the production and distribution of fakes necessarily depend upon a wide popular demand. That is why at the present moment, reproducers are largely concentrating on pattern glass. Fads and fakes always go hand in hand.

Some years ago when the craze was all for the more primitive forms of American antiques, it was natural that nondiscriminating fans should go in heavily for any old bottle that looked appropriate on the shelves of well-worn pine corner cupboards, or on the "period" mantels of dining rooms that aped seventeenth-century kitchens. The true collectors of historical flasks were, of course, a different class. They had the valuable help of Mr. Van Rensselaer's "Check List" of types, classifications and attributions and, moreover, sought and paid high for color and beauty as well as for rarity. For the mere faddists, any old-looking bottle sufficed, so they bought medicine vials, ink and bitters bottles; demijohns and pickle bottles and jars, large and small, and even huge carboys that had held acid, which, of course, was in harmony with the old-pine interior, as the Pilgrim Fathers habitually kept their supply of rum close to the hearth. Buyers were told, in strict confidence, that they must always look for the "pontil mark," which not only was the infallible test of antiquity but accounted for the high dollar values. The effectiveness of such pieces in creating the desired "atmosphere" was accepted without question by many of these American devotees.

At a quite early stage of the antique boom, large new pickle jars made their appearance. These were not necessarily copies or close imitations of old ones, but they were useful as flower holders, just as the smaller pickle bottles were made to serve as lamps. The electric light bulb, of course, reminded the proud owners of the lighting devices of the *Mayflower*'s passengers!

Among the earlier bottle reproductions was the tall log cabin Plantation Bitters, which was made in a beautiful blue and in a bright green. These were intended to be electrified for service as lamps. While they were doubtless copies from the well-known Drake's Plantation Bitters bottles, they did not have the blown letters of the original and no collector could have been fooled. Indeed, I do not recall that dealers ever sold or tried to sell them as old. Plate 28.

An active demand necessitates an adequate supply, if dealers are to stay in business. The moment genuine old bottles were no longer to be found in quantity in the old attics and virgin cellars that had been fine-tooth-combed by pickers and collectors, it became necessary to fall back on imitations and reproductions to supply the demand. After the fake pickle bottles and the Plantation Bitters, the first of the historical flasks appeared. Curiously enough, the makers selected one of the cheapest and most common of all the flasks in Van Rensselaer's Check List: the Cornucopia-Basket of Fruit flask. It may be doubted whether the makers actually intended it to be passed on to collectors as an antique, for it had an ornamental glass stopper and, in many gift shops, specimens were seen with gilding or hand-painted decorations in color. It would have been truer to form if the makers had furnished instead antique corncobs or discolored wooden plugs. Also it did not have the scarred base of the old ones. The new flasks came in a shade of reddish-brown amber which was not found in the originals. Most of the early Connecticut and New Hampshire bottles were made of inexpensive glass, and the olive-green, olive-amber and yellowish-brown amber in which the old flasks come may possibly be a more difficult color to imitate today than the amethyst, blue or puce for which collectors paid very high prices.

The new Cornucopia-Basket of Fruit flask did not sell well either because it was too common a pattern for a fake or because it was not pushed intensively. Not very long ago, one of these bottles, ornamental stopper and all, was sold as old at the auction sale in New York of a famous glass collection. Plate 29.

Copies of the so-called violin bottles were soon seen in many colors, such as ruby-red, sapphire-blue, amber, etc. The colors are too vivid, and the glass much too heavy. These and the new high-shouldered Sunburst bottles were made on order for a man in Boston. The initial of his last name, "M," may sometimes be discerned in the base of both bottles. The new mold carried this letter in it, but the scar left by the punty rod usually obliterated it, so it is rarely ever found today. The Sunburst bottles are good copies in some respects except for the usual flagrant errors; the glass is too clear; the colors too vivid and the glass usually, though not always, too heavy. Moreover, neither flask was made in red originally.

A quart flask having a cluster of grapes on one side, with an eagle on the reverse, in amber and in other colors, is frequently seen in gift shops. They are priced as low as $2.00. Originals are worth $15.00 in aquamarine and in amber would be worth more. I have seen them listed wholesale at $1.00.

A quart Washington with Eagle and 12 Stars has been reported in deep blue, which the owner describes as crudely blown. It was apparently produced from a plaster mold.

During the 1920's there appeared the Jenny Lind calabash bottle bearing the inscription FISLERVILLE GLASS WORKS. It was made in Haida, Czechoslovakia. A definite effort was made to copy the original, which, incidentally, never was a high-priced item, selling at from $5.00 to $10.00 in aquamarine. All varieties of Jenny Lind bottles were fairly popular years ago because they were easily identified with the period of the Swedish Nightingale's visit to America. That made them old enough to be considered antique by young collectors. Some unscrupulous dealers bought the reproduction and passed it on to customers at a profit of 300 per cent or better, but many more bought it believing it to be really old, because the pickers and runners who peddled them went to the trouble of carefully "antiquing" them with oil and inexpensive dirt and wear marks. All over New England, Pennsylvania and New York pickers planted many of them in barns and hen houses and showed many an honest farmer how to double his money the next time city slickers came around to rob him of his family heirlooms. The imitation differs in certain details from the original, but only a specialist in bottles would notice them. The neck, for example, does not taper quite like that of the old, and there are minor differences in wreath, bust and base, which may be detected, provided you know how and where to look. This particular fake did a great deal to kill the demand for all Jenny Lind calabash bottles. It is still found today in small shops, whose owners, unfortunately too numerous, believe that the customer should pay for the ignorance of dealers who bought as genuinely old what later turned out to be new and of little value. The Czechoslovakian copy may be seen on Plate 30, and a later South Jersey fake on Plate 31. The importers state that the Jenny Lind calabash is no longer made but a few years ago plenty of them were selling at 50¢ each.

Following the Czechoslovakian imports, a second edition was produced in South Jersey, in vivid shades of purple, emerald green, amber, and sapphire blue. The most startling one to come to light was shaded from red to amber, somewhat in the effect of New England's amberina. This particular variety of a Jenny Lind calabash bottle also carried, on the reverse side, a view of the Fislerville Glassworks.

There are two rather simple ways of distinguishing the new ones from the old. The copies have a pontil mark in the base which appears to have been stamped on, instead of the familiar rough scar left when the bottle was broken from the pontil rod. These rough scars are often sharp enough to cut the finger, but with most of the reproductions, the pontil marks are just fairly smooth, round depressions, often not even in the center of the base. The original Jenny Lind bottles have a fairly good-sized neck which tapers toward the top. The reproductions have a more slender neck which rises in straight lines, without tapering, from the body of the bottle. The modeling of the design is poor.

The fluted melon-shaped bottle is similar to an early Ohio type. The new one illustrated is Mexican, aquamarine in color, and filled with more tiny bubbles than would be found in old Ohio glass. There is little attempt to deceive, so far as the pontil scar is concerned, for the mark on the base shows only a faint round stamp. These bottles were sold in gift shops years ago, at $1.00 each. Plate 31.

A still later reproduction that sold fairly well until its spuriousness became a matter of common knowledge, was the flask with the Horse and Cart and the inscription SUCCESS TO THE RAILROAD. In some respects it was a good copy, but the makers again blundered on details and made it easy to distinguish it from the authentic. The most important of these were in the curve of the neck of the horse and particularly in the mane, which consisted of sharply defined short hairs that stood straight up. You could feel them with your fingers. Some dealers ground out the telltale mane but the marks of the grinding wheel show plainly. Of several variants of the authentic Horse and Cart flask, in all but one of them the mane droops over the side, as a decent horse's mane ought to do. The importer informed me that the mold cost $200 to make. Original Horse and Cart flasks are fairly common in various shades of amber but quite scarce in aquamarine. The new ones were made in several other colors in which originals never have been found. I show it as it appeared in the photograph the late Harry Hall White sent me. Plate 28.

Some time later, reproductions of the once greatly coveted E. C. Booz Old Cabin Whiskey 1840 bottle made their appearance. Rumors have it that an old glass blower in South Jersey found one of the original molds. This story is seriously doubted. If actually really true, it was reconditioned. More than likely a new one was made and so it became possible to turn out large quantities of Booz bottles. The original was a product of the Whitney Glass Works, not very far from where the reproductions have been made. The old bottles once sold as high as $150 for the amber and $300 for the green, but they never were justly entitled to the popularity they enjoyed because their history was based upon errors. One was the mistaken theory that the bottles were made during the Log Cabin and Hard Cider campaign of 1840. Again, it was asserted that the word "booze" was derived from the name of the Philadelphia whisky dealer, Mr. Booz, though as a matter of fact it was Elizabethan English. Despite the fact that the reproductions were made from a good mold, the quality of the glass betrayed their newness in the amber specimen and in the shade of the color in the green. Moreover, there was no period after the word "Whiskey," as is found in the old. Before it was generally known that it was being reproduced and honestly sold by the maker at reproduction prices, a number of experienced dealers paid high for the copies. For many years a brisk demand had existed for the Booz bottles, showing the persistence of error, because it was the myth that sold them. The price subsequently fell considerably from the boom-time top. Today it may be doubted whether any but an inexperienced collector would have the courage to pay more than a few dollars for a genuine Booz bottle. Plate 32. About twelve years later a reproduction of the Booz bottle with the roof ridge beveled at the ends appeared. It is a very poor imitation.

The pint flask shown on Plate 29 has a bust of Washington with the inscription, THE FATHER OF HIS COUNTRY on one side and exactly the same on the reverse. No such bottle exists among the genuine historical flasks. The color in some is almost the smoky shade of the cheap sunglasses sold in the "five and tens," and the surface is rough, almost crinkled. Possibly it was intended thereby to differentiate it from ordinary smooth-surfaced commercial containers. The bust is not a good copy of any seen on the old Washington flasks. The hair, the nose, the flat base and the lettering betray the newness the moment you look at it. Since it is obviously not a reproduction, it may not be fair to class it with the fakes. In 1932, the bicentenary of Washington's birth, many commemorative articles came on the market, among them being the quart bottles sold in chain stores as vinegar containers. These displayed a bust of Washington. The novelty Washington bottles were too unattractive for the gift shops to handle successfully, while antique dealers and pickers refused to buy them because no one could mistake them for old. A calabash-shaped bottle bearing the same bust as on Plate 29, was also made. It was even worse as a reproduction. The neck is too thick; the base is flat and the bottle is larger than the old ones. The glass is the same as in the flask. It is seldom one finds either of these on sale in any kind of shop today, though occasionally they appear on dealers' lists, without enlightening descriptions. Plate 30.

Later came a pint flask with a bust of George Washington and the inscription WASHINGTON on one side and on the reverse, a bust of Taylor with the inscription GEN. Z. TAYLOR. It was made in Haida, Czechoslovakia, where the Jenny Lind, Fislerville, calabash reproductions originated. Again serious mistakes were made, easily recognizable by anyone familiar with authentic historical flasks. The busts show differences and, moreover, the flask was produced in colors that are not found in the old. These strange

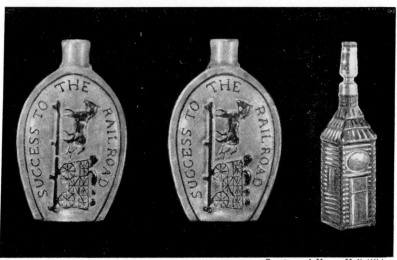

Courtesy of Harry Hall White.

Plate 28
FAKE HORSE AND CART—"SUCCESS TO THE RAILROAD."
FAKE PLANTATION BITTERS BOTTLE.

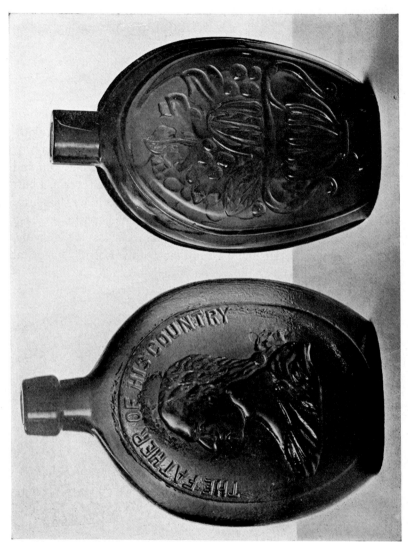

Plate 29

Plate 30
FAKE FISLERVILLE JENNY LIND MADE IN CZECHOSLOVAKIA
AND NEW WASHINGTON "CALABASH" BOTTLE.

Plate 31

SOUTH JERSEY COPY OF JENNY LIND.   MODERN LACY PLATE.   MEXICAN BOTTLE.

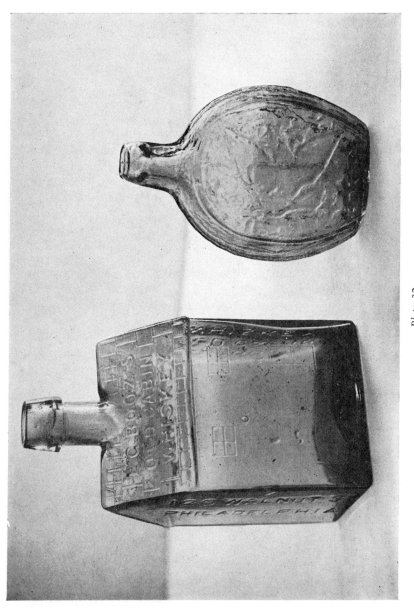

Plate 32

OLD LOG CABIN BOOZ BOTTLE.   LOWELL RAILROAD—EAGLE, FAKE.

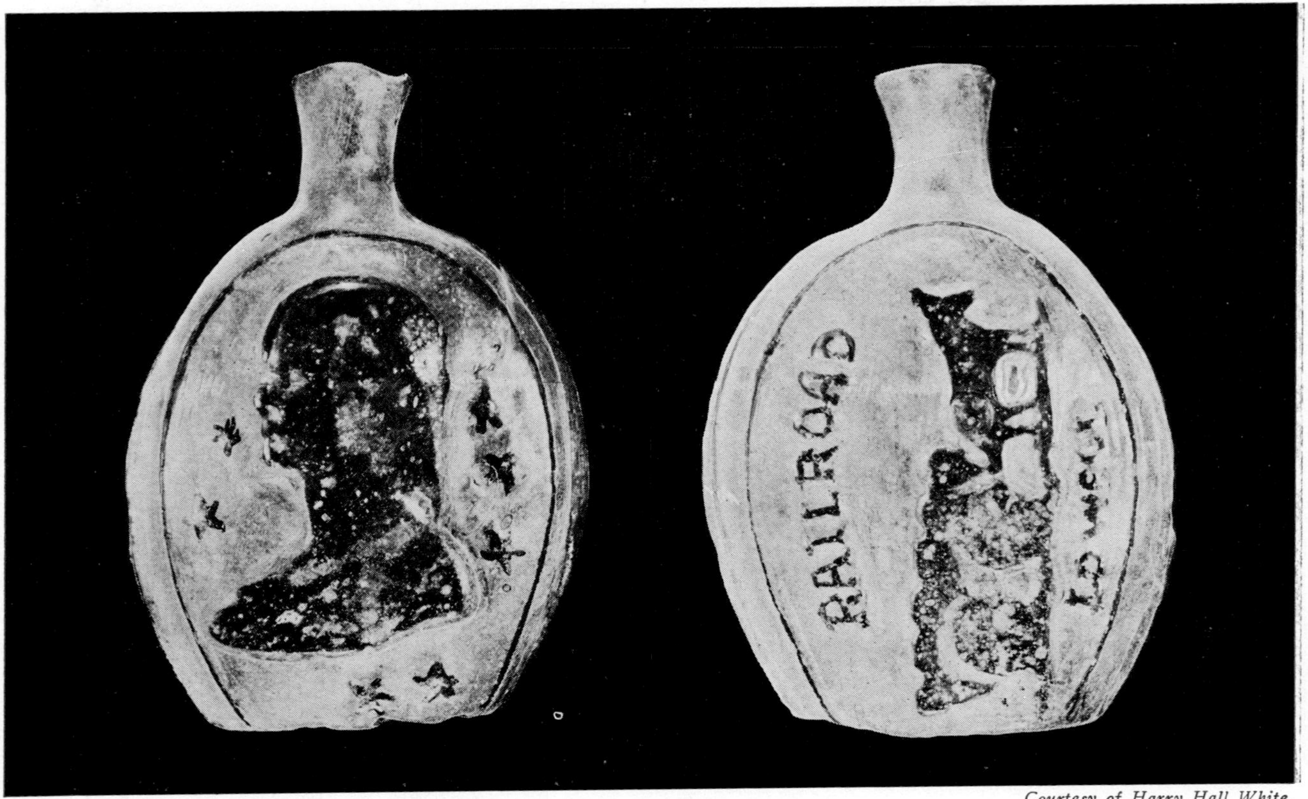

Courtesy of *Harry Hall White.*

Plate 33

LOWELL RAILROAD, REVERSE, WASHINGTON.

shades, instead of inducing purchases, really put otherwise unsuspecting collectors on their guard. This particular flask, when genuine, usually comes in aquamarine and is seldom seen in any of the colors which other varieties of old Washington-Taylor flasks show. Of course, inexpert collectors unsuspectingly bought the new ones. Its chief accomplishment has been to make both collectors and the smaller dealers skeptical about the authenticity of many genuine flasks. After all, it is not always easy to distinguish fakes from originals. The importers say they have discontinued this line but they are still offered for sale at the smaller shops.

A still later fake is a half-pint with an outspread eagle on one side and on the reverse, a Horse and Cart, lettered Lowell and Railroad. It certainly is not a true reproduction made from a good new mold. It resembles the fakes that turned up in Philadelphia a few years ago, made from plaster of Paris molds. The Lowell-Railroad half-pint is very crude, so badly misshapen and blurred that it could not possibly pass for authentic. Nevertheless, some dealers bought them. As a rule they sold at a very low price. Most of them are light green with a slight yellowish cast, but they also come in shades unlike any seen in the original, which were mostly olive-green or the familiar golden-amber. One turned up in a brilliant sapphire blue. Another Lowell Railroad half-pint "variant" has a bust of Washington on the reverse. No such flask was made originally. It cannot be called an imitation. These are the crudest flasks ever made, as may be seen from the illustrations on Plates 32 and 33. They were produced by an individual workman in New Jersey, in the 1930's.

The experiment of using plaster of Paris molds to make flasks is not new. Years ago, a few of these crude, misshapen, poorly impressed flasks made their appearance in some of the Pine Street antique shops of Philadelphia. Before that, I had seen a quart in a deep opaque-blue in a New York shop where it was held at $150. A well-known collector has a half-pint of the Albany Glass Works, Washington on one side and a ship on the reverse, and also a quart, Eagle, with cluster of grapes on the reverse. The latter was found in a Pine Street shop by another famous bottle collector. The dealer from whom the fake was bought told the collector that the man who made it was a workman at a glass factory in New Jersey, not very far from Philadelphia, who blew it after hours out of impure glass, which cost him nothing. These pieces were made in all sorts of freak colors, for the blowers used what was left in the pots at the end of the day.

Probably the best copy of an old historical flask is the Dyottville, Washington-Taylor. However, even this one should not fool a discriminating bottle collector. The colors are not only exceedingly poor, but the pontil mark on the base has been molded in, instead of being left scarred. The distinguishing feature of the reproductions is the difference in the inscription PHILAD^A. On the originals, the *a* is smaller than the other letters and it is not on the same line with them. On the reproductions the letters are uniform in size and on the same line.

The only fake historical flasks which are sometimes sold as original by unscrupulous dealers, as far as I know, are those I have described. Of course, there are also the large Cathedral pickle jars and the Moses type of Spring Water bottle in a beautiful green. The latter can be obtained in the same green glass that was used to make reproductions of the large barrel-shaped bottles which, years ago, came to this country from France with some sort of tamarind preserves. Glass pieces of this type are used by interior decorators in certain color schemes. They have been converted into lamps that are decidedly attractive. I once saw a very large demijohn, in the inside of which was an elaborate cluster of small electric bulbs. It undoubtedly took time and skill to electrify that chandelier.

No attempt has been made to include the reproductions of "freak" bottles, like glass cigars, revolvers, busts of persons known and unknown to fame, etc., since the oldest of the originals are not very old. All of them, new or old, are priced too low to make it worth while warning curio buyers.

The flask collector has not had much to worry about. The imitations of the early blown diamond-quilted and other such patterns did the most harm and they are treated and illustrated here. For the convenience of collectors, a list of the new flasks is appended to the end of this chapter, together with their respective chart numbers from George and Helen McKearin's *American Glass*.

BLOWN PATTERN-MOLDED BOTTLES

The first half-pint, amethyst diamond-quilted fake bottle to cause havoc among serious collectors was not made in South Jersey (Plate 34), but came from Czechoslovakia and, I was informed, sold wholesale for $6 at the start. The ultimate consumer was invited to buy it at "bargain prices" that ranged from $250 to $300. They are too heavy. The neck is not right. The diamond-quilting is so thick as to appear pressed instead of being the finely blown and expanded diamond it was supposed to be. Compare it (Plate 34), with the genuine old one shown on Plate 35. Even in the pictures the difference is noticeable. It is much more clearly seen in the actual specimens. Nevertheless it did considerable harm.

From Czechoslovakia, and of the same period as the bottle just described, also came the heavier diamond-patterned flask shown first on the left of Plate 36. It will be noted that it exhibits the same type of workmanship as the first one. It appeared in a deep sapphire blue instead of amethyst. These are the only two imported bottles of this type to come to the attention of the writer. The entire base of the blue bottle pictured was ground down to suggest the wear of age. It would take a million years of shelf-rubbing to wear it down to that extent.

These fakes came on the market about 1930. Three midwestern dealers decided to sell them over a large area, and they apparently co-ordinated their operations. Early on the same morning, so that there would be no opportunity for discussion among the selected victims, one man sent day letters from Toledo to a large number of well-known dealers and collectors throughout the country to this effect: I AM INFORMED YOU ARE INTERESTED IN RARE FLASKS. KINDLY ADVISE IF YOU WOULD LIKE ME TO SHIP YOU AN AME-THYST DIAMOND-QUILTED TOILET BOTTLE, EXPRESS C.O.D., SUB-

JECT TO EXAMINATION, AT THREE HUNDRED DOLLARS. He himself was not known as a dealer. It caught a good many, for it was a cleverly planned maneuver, which the plotters figured would fool many collectors, in particular those who are always on the watch for "variants." Sure enough several paid the "bargain price." There could be no legal redress, because, after all, there was no technical misrepresentation and the buyer did have an opportunity to examine the piece. If inveterate bargain hunters thought it was rarer than the familiar Stiegels that sold at $500 to $1000, it was their funeral. I did not wire for one, but I know many who did. Some promptly shipped the flask back. Others sent checks. One smart collector let the box stay in the express office after he had refused to take it. The would-be seller wrote and wired, reducing the price several times, but as it did not decline to $2.00, the wise collector, being Pennsylvania Dutch, did not buy it.

Along about 1935, blown flasks were being produced in South Jersey, contemporaneously with the lily pad bowls, pitchers, creamers, etc. and were made by the same individual who did the copies of the early blown glass. These South Jersey reproductions, which are fully illustrated here, were blown in a workshop located in the rear of his home. From individual specimens of high-class art work, he turned to blue, amethyst, and emerald-green imitations of Stiegel and Ohio Stiegel types. These cannot be called exact copies of early American examples. It is possible that the maker may have been prompted by suggestions from some antique dealer who saw profitable possibilities for himself. It may, of course, be merely a coincidence that some of the first of the new "South Jersey Stiegels" turned up in Ohio, too far away from the source of the supply to arouse suspicion as to the real reason for the bargain prices of the "rare items."

At the time I visited the workshop of the glassworker in South Jersey, in the mid-1930's, his line included diamond-quilted bottles in all sizes from miniatures to full pints in amethyst and other colors; blown bottles in fine shades of color in swirled effects, as well as one in a broken-column design. These may all be seen on Plates 7, 11, 36, 37, 38 and the frontispiece. The bottle on the

Plate 34
CZECHOSLOVAKIAN FAKE MARKETED YEARS AGO.

Plate 35
GENUINE STIEGEL DIAMOND-QUILTED BOTTLE.

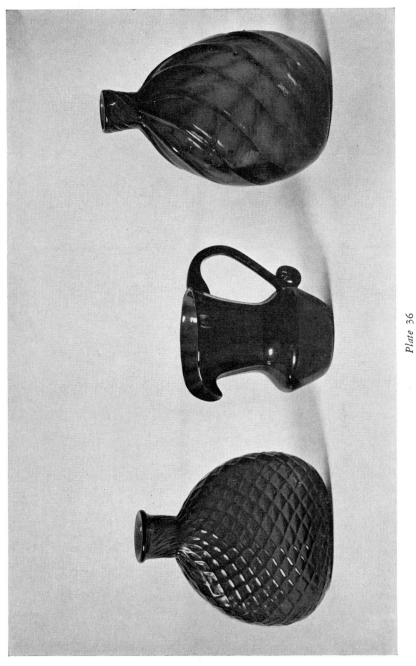

Plate 36

CZECHOSLOVAKIAN BOTTLE ON LEFT. ON RIGHT, TWO SOUTH JERSEY FAKES.

Plate 37

MODERN SOUTH JERSEY BOTTLES.

Plate 38

MODERN SOUTH JERSEY BOTTLES.

right end of Plate 37 was made from an English mold which he claimed to be about seventy-five years old.

None of the new amethyst or other colored Jersey reproductions really resemble the old ones closely enough to make them appear genuine when placed side by side. Even though you find particles of sand and some bubbles in them and wear marks are seen on the base, with a fairly deceptive pontil thrown in for good measure, they still are far from even looking right.

Pictured on Plate 15 is one of the most curious bottles in imitation of blown three-mold glass that have come to light so far. It attracted my attention in the window of an antique shop because of its beautiful color—a brilliant, clear amethyst. Like other reproductions of blown three-mold, it is a poor copy of this type of early glass. It is a half-pint size, complete with a stopper patterned after those used in the familiar ribbed or swirled vinegar bottles. The base is very flat, with a pressed (or stamped) impression which is supposed to represent a pontil mark. The bottle itself has a narrow row of vertical ribbing. About the center of the bottle are three large sunbursts, alternating with what must be taken to represent diamond-quilting. The design is so thin that it looks more like four-pointed stars or the old-fashioned cross-stitching. Above this broad band is more diagonal ribbing. Vertical ribbing runs from this point into the neck of the bottle. On a genuine piece, the impression would be clearly defined. The owner told me he paid $2.00 for it, and that three customers had rejected it at $8.00! The rejections may be regarded as encouraging if they indicate a growing wariness on the part of buyers. This bottle would not deceive the average collector, but one may well wonder if in years to come such pieces may not find their way into select collections. It is the unawareness of the existence of new fakes that often trips up even old collectors who love to swoop down on what at first sight appears to be a "rare variant." Why "freaks" should have the appeal they seem to possess for rabid collectors is a mystery to those of us who prefer consistent, careful workmanship and adherence to the best traditions of bygone days, when craftsmanship counted.

REPRODUCTION FLASKS
Group numbers from McKearin's *American Glass*

1. G1—No. 29   "Albany Glass Works," over ship. Very poor mold work and colors. Half-pint. Letter *N* in New York is reversed. Seam on one side indicates cracked mold.

2. G1—No. 37   "Dyottville," Washington-Taylor. Probably the best of the fakes except for the pontil on base (which is molded in) and the colors, which are extremely bad. Also, uniformity of lettering is incorrect. See text.

3. G1—No. 107   Fislerville, Jenny Lind. Early Czechoslovakian copy. Very poor.

4. G1—No. 107   Fislerville, Jenny Lind. Later South Jersey copy. Very poor. Differences may be noted in the illustrations.

5. G2—No. 46   Eagle—Cornucopia. Fairly good. Half-pint.

6. G2—No. 55   Eagle—Cluster of Grapes. Fairly good. It is possible that some copies were imports, made from metal mold, and others produced in South Jersey, possibly from plaster molds.

7. G III—6 No. 205   Cornucopia—Basket of Fruit. First copy made early for gift shops. Later copy much better. Pint.

8. G V—5   Success to the Railroad, Horse and Cart. Mold work better than on most. About ten years ago another reproduction came out which is entirely different and very poor. The horse is a weird-looking animal, very thin bodied.

9. G5—No. 10   Lowell-Railroad. From plaster mold, very poor.

10. G VII—3 No. 281   Booz bottles. Good copies except those in unusual colors, not made originally. Later, type with roof ridge beveled at ends ap-

		peared, in a very poor copy. This is G VII—4, No. 282.
11.	G VIII—2 No. 286	High-shouldered Sunburst. Rather good except glass is too clear and colors too vivid. It is also seen now in colors never used originally.
12.	G I—49	Pint, bust of "Washington," reverse, bust inscribed GEN. Z. TAYLOR. Czechoslovakia. Produced in colors not found in the old.
13.	G IX—10 No. 325	Pint violin. Glass much too heavy and colors too vivid. Again colors were made that were never used originally.
14.		Lowell-Railroad "variant" has a bust of Washington on reverse. No such old flask was made. Plaster mold. Very poor.
15.		Quart, Washington, reverse, Eagle with 12 stars. This has been reported but I have not seen it.
16.		Half-pint, bluish-aquamarine cornucopia, reverse, basket of flowers. Reported, but I have not seen it.
17.		Washington—Sheaf of Rye. Made from plaster mold.
18.		Pint, Washington, both sides Plate 29.
19.		Calabash, with bust of Washington, lettered, THE FATHER OF HIS COUNTRY. Plate 30.
20.	G I—28	Pint, "Albany Glass Works." From a plaster mold, in various colors.

Also blown three-mold flasks, with sunburst, in pint and half-pint sizes, in clear and in color.

Chapter V

REPRODUCTION AND SOUVENIR CUP PLATES

Reproductions in cup plates cannot be considered a serious threat to collectors today, because there are so few of them. Exactly ten have been produced in this country up to 1948. It is a simple enough matter to detect the new ones, because there is no ring to the glass. Of course one must know how to go about testing them. By holding the cup plates securely in the center with the thumb on one side and the forefinger on the other, with no other part of the hand touching the glass, it is easy to tap it with a pencil or any metallic object and listen for the telltale sound. In the case of most old plates, there is a clear resounding ring. From the new plates, one hears a flat, deadened thud. While there are some old cup plates that were made from window or bottle glass and therefore do not have a bell tone, it so happens that any of the plates which have been copied so far *do* ring in the originals. The great harm reproductions do to new collectors is to make them suspicious of every plate. Many good pieces are rejected which really are authentic, thereby nipping in the bud more than one promising collector.

The first fake to come on the market was the Henry Clay facing to the left with a star under the bust. It appeared along about 1922 or 1923. Aside from the fact that it does not ring, there are minor differences in the design. The lettering is smaller, the letters having plain ends. The scrolls in the center and all border designs are lighter and skimpy. The lettering of "Henry" is too small and the "Clay" too large. This plate was a copy of our No. 565-B.* It was made in blue, as well as in clear glass.

The next reproduction of a Henry Clay appeared in recent years and attempts to copy our No. 564. The chief differences are in the

* *American Glass Cup Plates* by Ruth Webb Lee and James H. Rose.

75

Plate 39
FOUR REPRODUCTION CUP PLATES.

plain ends of the letters, which are bereft of serifs. The bust is
that of a boy with a receding chin, small nose and high rounding
forehead. This plate appeared in pink and in clear glass.

For some strange reason, the Henry Clay was again chosen as a
plate to copy in France, apparently for export to this country. One
may be seen in Plate 39 with the paper label MADE IN FRANCE
prominently displayed. It was produced in several colors, including light blue, pink and a deep salmon shade. Should the paper
label be removed, this plate is still easy to detect aside from its
nonringing quality. There are many discrepancies in the design.
The head is shaped differently from that in any of our old ones,

having a more prominent forehead. The lettering is smaller, the star under the bust is smaller and the dots surrounding the bust are very light. The shields in the border are noticeably much too shallow. The serrations on the edge are large and even. Old serrations are never absolutely even. The same serration error may also be noted in the copy of No. 565-B on Plate 39.

Along about 1923 the first reproduction of the ship *Benjamin Franklin* appeared. It was made at this time in sapphire blue and in clear glass. There are a number of discrepancies in the design but, even so, the workmanship is better than in the more recent copies.

Plate 40
FOUR REPRODUCTION CUP PLATES.

Plate 41
THREE REPRODUCTION CUP PLATES.

The older fraud (Plate 40) shows slight waves under the boat, whereas they are heavy on the original plate. The bell is entirely different in the new, and the cable cord surrounding the center is heavier. There are minor discrepancies in the design, such as: the plain ends of the letters, that is, no serif; and no walking beam over the paddle wheel. Some of the details in the old are missing in the new.

Some seven or eight years later, another copy of the ship *Benjamin Franklin* was produced by the Westmoreland Glass Company. Their product may also be seen on Plate 40, adorned with their company paper label. In the old plate the stippling has a silvery sheen, while there is no luster to the new. The rope rigging appears to be rope in the original, but is hardly more than a rippled line on the new. The same evenness of the scalloped edge is apparent. As stated before, these are never exactly even on the old. The lettering is better on the Westmoreland copy than in the earlier (1923) version.

The first of the epidemic of new cup plates made during the early 1930's was a copy of the Butterfly, pictured on Plate 40. It was made by a midwestern factory on order for a private party in central New York State, who paid fifty dollars for the mold. The whole country was flooded with them in clear glass and in colors. Many were sold in gift shops for 35¢ to 50¢ each.

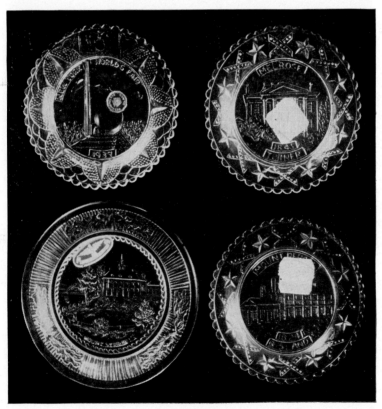

Plate 42
FOUR MODERN SOUVENIR CUP PLATES.

Plate 43

TWO MODERN WASHINGTON SOUVENIR CUP PLATES.

Open-edge dish not a true cup plate. Odd plate at lower right is old but ground off.

We are not certain that the next series of six plates was made to special order. It is more likely that the factory, seeing how quickly the Butterflies flew into antique shops, decided to make a few other varieties on their own. At any rate, the Bunker Hill, Thirteen Hearts, the Henry Clay with star under the bust, dated 1831 Eagle, and the Before and After Marriage, as well as the Benjamin Franklin previously described, all appeared in rapid succession. A Butterfly plate in a toddy size, which was never made originally, appeared in gift shops at this period. Plate 162.

The Butterfly reproduction has the usual discrepancies in workmanship. In the new, the stems of the two leaves on each sprig are almost directly opposite each other and each flower has six petals. On the old, the stems of the leaves are at least one-eighth inch apart and one flower has seven petals. The stippling in the background is too coarse and mechanical. Arrows point to errors in the design on Plate 40.

The copy of the Thirteen Hearts plate is the most obviously new of any of the reproductions. The smaller, more pointed hearts in the border are so widely separated as to resemble the twelve-heart cup plate. It rests on a plain rim instead of a rope rim. Apparently two molds have been made because the stippling in the earlier one is finer. One is shown on Plate 40.

Of all the fakes, the dated 1831 Eagle, shown on Plate 41, is by far the best. The nonringing quality of the glass is a quick, sure test of the reproduction. The old dated Eagles have seventy-eight or seventy-nine serrations. The new have seventy-nine. There are noticeable small differences in minor details of the border. Also, in the new the upper portion of the Eagle's legs appears in heavier outline and they are slightly larger. The chief difference between the old and the new dated Eagle plate is in the clarity of the design. The old one was done by a moldmaker whose work shows more care and precision. The result was a finished product showing sharpness of detail. So far the copies have appeared only in clear glass.

Copies of the Bunker Hill cup plate have been widely distributed via gift shops and department stores. The arrows on the illustration of the copy point to numerous means of identifying the fake. The serrations on the border are too even. They are never so exactly regular in the originals. The tassels at the ends of each drape are missing. The lettering is plain, without serifs, and is noticeably much too large. The monument adorning the center of the plate is much taller and bigger in the new and the bricks in the monument are larger. So far this reproduction has only appeared in clear glass. It is shown on Plate 41.

The Before and After Marriage cup plate is an amusing subject and the manufacturers of the copy undoubtedly figured it would have a wide sale. Collectors of cup plates who take their hobby seriously develop a practiced eye for small details, so when the new plates appear in antique shops, they are not easily deceived. The old plate is three and a half inches in diameter, while the new is three and three-eighths inches. The fake has dots in between the lettering, while the old has dots or stars. Plate 41. This reproduction is a copy of our No. 698.

In the case of the old Valentine cup plate, the stippling is heavier and more evenly distributed than on the new. The original is heavier and, of course, has a good, clear ring when tapped. The new Valentine has a thinner stippling, which is thicker and heavier in some spots than in others. The design does not have the same depth or brilliance. Then, too, the old plate is a trifle smaller than the new. The reproduction is shown on Plate 39.

Confusing to new collectors is a series of commemorative plates which have historical significance but are strictly modern. Four of these plates are shown on Plate 42 and two others on Plate 43.

In the upper left-hand corner of Plate 42 is a New York World's Fair souvenir which is so marked and dated 1939. The center design in the base pictures the sphere and trylon, familiar to all those who attended the Fair. Probably all this series of plates was planned to serve a double purpose—a souvenir to take home which was readily adaptable to use as an ash tray.

The cup plate in the upper right-hand corner of Plate 42 is marked and dated, MELROSE—1845—TURNER. It has been said that these were souvenirs sold at a garden festival in Natchez, Miss.

Beneath the plate just described, in the lower right-hand corner, is a similar one showing a building in the center and marked MOUNT REPOSE—1824—BISLAND.

At the lower left is a modern plate which may be another from a World's Fair series. It carries a paper label inscribed, HISTORICAL AMERICA. In the center is a view of Mount Vernon, marked accordingly. The border is ribbed and carries a design of acorns and oak leaves.

Not illustrated is another souvenir plate of the Golden Gate World's Fair in California.

Confusing to new collectors are two Washington cup plates which are not reproductions but purely commemorative pieces. These are both shown on Plate 43. It will be noted that one is marked G. WASHINGTON, 1732–1799 and the other is marked "G. Washington, 1732–1932." Obviously, one carries the dates of his birth and death, and the other honors the two-hundredth anniversary of the birth of the Father of Our Country. It is thought that these were also a World's Fair souvenir.

In the lower row of Plate 43 at the right is a cup plate with the scalloped edge ground smooth. Some unsuspecting collector might well come across such a plate, always found with a serrated edge, and feel he had found an unknown variant. It is always well to scrutinize such an oddity with care.

In the lower left-hand corner of Plate 43 is a little, open chain-bordered three-and-a-quarter-inch item which is not a true cup plate, though some have been added to collections as such. It is not a reproduction of an old piece because it is modern. It is simply not a cup plate.

Some of the fakes often have artificial age marks added, such as the chip on the Henry Clay on Plate 39. Besides the many distinguishing characteristics of old and new, as noted, remember that the quality of the glass tells the story. At least it does on the ten copied to date in this country, for any of the originals should have an unmistakable ring to the glass.

In particular, collectors and dealers should not be discouraged by reading advertisements stating that cup plates are being made from original molds. The following appeared in the Boston *Herald* one bright morning in 1947, accompanied by a photograph of reproductions of seven old cup plates plus a modern Washington souvenir plate, pictured on our Plate 43. The quotation is exact:

Lacy Sandwich Glass. Precious Little Cup Plates (measurements 3¼″ in diameter). You'll find every one of these listed in the antique glass books. They are currently produced from old molds—even an expert has trouble telling the old ones from these of modern day.

Left to right—top row by names: Benjamin Franklin, Bunker Hill, Henry Clay, Butterfly. Bottom row—The Wedding Day and Three Weeks Later, Hearts and Darts, Washington, 1831 Eagle. 8 Assorted to set. $2.50 set.

The "Hearts and Darts" refers to the Valentine. All the reproductions are pictured in this chapter.

A letter to the Boston Better Business Bureau protesting the statements that these cup plates were made from old molds and that even an expert would have difficulty in telling them from the old brought an equally prompt reply from the bureau stating an investigation had been made and that the writer was correct. The letter stated further that the store under whose name the advertising appeared had acted on information given them by the agent selling them the cup plates and that the glass would not be advertised again in the same manner. A great deal of damage was done, but at least it was stopped quickly. Collectors and dealers alike would be doing an infinite amount of good by reporting to their local chambers of commerce or better business bureaus, any similar misstatements.

This chapter appeared first in 1938 in *Antique Fakes and Reproductions*. It was rewritten and added to *American Glass Cup Plates* by Ruth Webb Lee and James H. Rose in 1948.

Chapter VI

PATTERN GLASS REPRODUCTIONS

There are now more reproductions of pattern glass than of any other small antiques, when one considers the relatively few years in which pattern glass has had a widespread appeal. Naturally, perpetrators of frauds seek the field which promises the biggest profit. It always has been true that active and widespread demand creates a supply and when originals are lacking substitutes make up the deficiency. There will always be copyists and imitators who do not tell the truth about the antiquity of their work.

Appended to this chapter is a list of all the pieces reproduced in the earlier patterns about which it has been possible for me to obtain the necessary data. There is also a list of items which bear some resemblance to old designs and for that reason confuse new collectors. Many modern gift shop pieces often find their way under false pretenses into antique shops, but I cannot attempt to describe or list the infinitude of things that people may consider worth collecting, irrespective of their age or usefulness, especially in these days when it is not necessary for items to be one hundred years old to be classed as genuinely antique or listed as "Americana."

In the list of reproductions, I have in each case tried to approximate as closely as possible the length of time that these copies have been on the market. Time, as much as the artificial abrasion to indicate wear, and other methods of aging glass, are factors not to be overlooked. I regard it as fortunate that I am able to list and illustrate items, made both here and abroad for distribution in this country during the past three decades, when the high peak of fakes was reached. I cannot assert that I have found all the copies produced during that time, for not all were extensively sold, but it is reasonably certain that very few have been missed. Such a book as this ought to be accessible as soon as possible to all collectors and dealers who should know what they must guard against today.

The first reproduction to cause consternation among the older collectors was the Turkey jam jar, which came out in the early 1920's. This piece was apparently used most frequently as a family sugar bowl originally but it has become known over the years as a jam jar. In my possession is an old trade catalogue showing this jar, which was then made in clear glass and also in clear, painted over with natural colors. The first copies came out in amber, light green, salmon pink and in blue, besides clear glass. Later on the Turkey jars appeared in a small size, never made originally. Again, years later, copies of the Turkey in an intermediate size were seen in ten-cent stores, priced at 39¢. The earliest reproductions were imported from Czechoslovakia by a small New York importing company.

More serious alarm was brought about in 1933 or 1934, when the same concern brought out the Horn of Plenty reproduction of the water tumbler. They then sold at 50¢ each. It was the first copy of any importance in the field of pattern glass. Today we are becoming so inured to the appearance of new pieces that it causes more irritation than shock.

The new Horn of Plenty water tumblers are fairly good copies but would not deceive a careful buyer. While the old tumblers have little ring to the glass when tapped, due to the shape, still a flint quality may be detected. The new tumbler has no ring, the saw-tooth part of the design is too sharp; and in place of the properly ground-out pontil, there is a rounded depression. Some time later these copies appeared in amber. Still later, freaks produced from the new tumbler mold were seen, as shown on Plate 44.

In recent years ugly copies of a large Horn of Plenty lamp bowl have appeared, the bowl in dark blue or in clear glass, usually mounted on milk-white bases.

The Star with Dewdrop salt was among the next of the more important reproductions. They were good enough copies to make collectors refrain from buying any of these salts because it was so difficult to tell the new from the old. Even an experienced eye failed to detect a difference, basically because there was always an element of doubt as to whether the piece used for comparison with an unquestioned new one was after all genuinely old. However, there are differences! Just between the scallop and the rim there is an almost invisible line in the new one which is absent in the old. It is like a slight indentation, caused by the new mold. The star in the genuine is slightly smaller because the dewdrops are smaller. Around the star in the base is a band formed by three rows of dewdrops. This band is narrower in the old, also because the dewdrops are smaller. Originally these salts were made only in crystal, but they are found in a number of colors today, including salmon-pink, apple-green and amethyst. The new ones may also be found with attached handles, thus forming a basket.

The president of a well-known glass company told me, a number of years ago, that he was approached by a private party who painted in glowing colors a picture of the enormous sale the reproduction of the Star with Dewdrop plate would have by reason of its great popularity. The president was in a receptive frame of mind and one "batch" * of the plates was made up, in the seven-and-one-quarter-inch size. Collectors and dealers, ever on the alert for new pieces, immediately stopped buying them. Department stores do not care to handle odd items and so there was no such sale of the plates as had been promised. When the head of the glass company realized that he had listened to poor advice, he stopped making them. Years later they reappeared in color, so perhaps the mold was sold. On the old one, there is a fairly wide rim on the base, which is sharp enough as it slopes toward the center to catch the fingernail. On the new one, this rim slopes smoothly toward the center. Plate 46.

Wildflower goblet reproductions came out first in apple-green. Because the demand for this color was the most active, the green goblets commanded the highest price. I am told that one dealer advertised five of these on a list. Ten collectors in and near one large city each ordered five. Fifty goblets! So hard to find before and then, by magic, so plentiful! One by one as the collectors met

* A batch usually means 250.

they began to compare notes and soon discovered discrepancies that revealed the sordid story. The shade of green was more blue-green in the new ones. The design was thinner (less heavily stippled) and the leaves and flowers seemed to vary. Moreover, the new one had a narrower fluting around the base of the bowl of the goblet, than is found on the old one. Some buyers returned the goblets, and their money was refunded. Later on the frauds appeared from a new mold, and this time the design was too heavy—too compact. They were made in all the original colors, but the shades were not as soft and mellow. The latest copy is shown on Plate 47.

New Wildflower square plates in blue, amber, yellow and clear glass have added to the general confusion. These vary in detail, as may be seen in the illustration on Plate 48. Scratches often show on a border panel of the reproductions.

The Westward-Ho goblet made its initial appearance, as nearly as I can recall, in the early part of 1936. At first glance they seemed rather good copies, but it was maddening to see so many dealers and collectors deceived into paying high prices for them. They were planted first through Pennsylvania by certain pickers who went about peddling them from a car. They always sold odd numbers of goblets, such as five or seven, wrapped up in old newspapers. As much as $10.00 each was paid for a fraud now selling at 75¢ to the trade. In more recent years, copies of the goblet in amethyst and in blue appeared. They were never made in color originally.

The authentic Westward-Ho pattern was designed by a man named Jacobus, who was associated with Gillinder & Sons, of Philadelphia, and who ranked as one of the best of his day. On Plate 49 compare the detail of the deer's body, the deer's mouth and the foliage, with the copy. It will be noted on the old one that every hair on the deer is as clearly defined as in an engraving. The deer's mouth is always a straight sealed line in the originals. In the new, the deer's body is decidedly mangy; in fact, almost devoid of hair. The mouth is blurred, as if the deer were chewing on the foliage. There are many other discrepancies in detail but these two

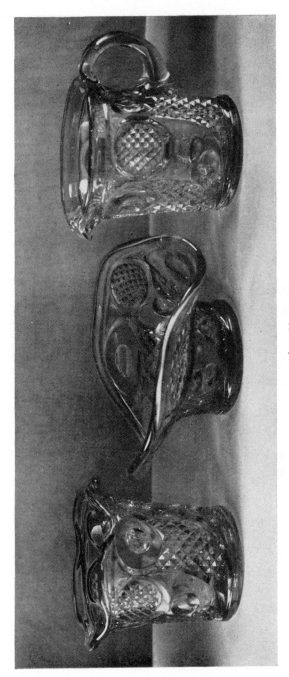

Plate 44

OBJECTS PRODUCED FROM NEW HORN OF PLENTY TUMBLER MOLD.

Plate 45

NEW OVERLAY TUMBLER—DAISY AND BUTTON HAND VASE—HORN OF PLENTY TUMBLER.

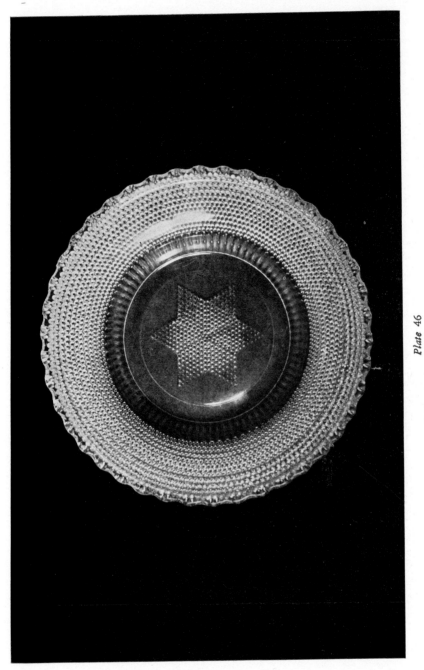

Plate 46

STAR WITH DEWDROP SEVEN-AND-ONE-QUARTER-INCH PLATE.

Plate 47

REPRODUCTION WILDFLOWER GOBLET IS ON THE RIGHT.

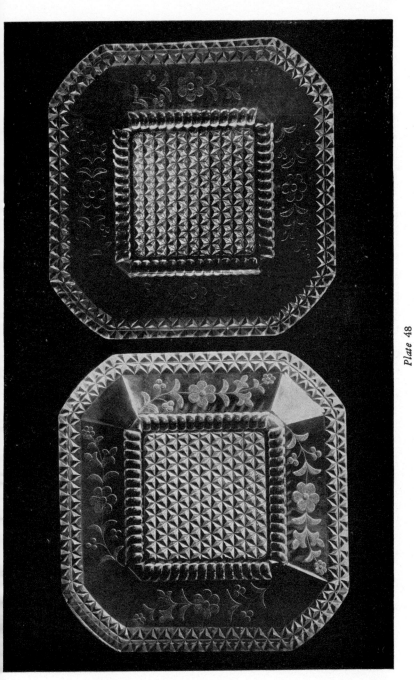

Plate 48

REPRODUCTION WILDFLOWER PLATE IS ON THE RIGHT.
THE DESIGN ON LATEST COPIES IS MUCH HEAVIER.

Plate 49

REPRODUCTION WESTWARD-HO GOBLET IS ON THE RIGHT.

Plate 50
WESTWARD-HO LAMP MADE FROM NEW GOBLET MOLD.
REPRODUCTION DOLPHIN COMPOTE.

failings will easily inform the buyer which not to buy as old. The first batch of Westward-Ho goblets evidenced a yellowish cast to the glass, while the frosting on those that followed was much too white. The old frosted finish is actually a gray-white. All the colored goblets are modern, as this pattern was made only in clear.

New Westward-Ho sauce dishes came out next, in the four-inch size. These were followed by a lamp which was converted from the reproduction goblet mold. Lamps were never made in this pattern originally. The new one may be seen on Plate 50. After World War II, the oval covered compote was made in the small size, on a low foot, and a round covered compote on a high foot, as well as wine glasses in the four-and-one-half-inch size. These all have common failings; that is, the frosting is too white and the detail of the design very poor, compared with the originals. A story reached me that the Westward-Ho water pitcher was made up for an unscrupulous dealer, who was given control of the mold. This is an old tale and one which has been repeated many times over. The glass company made a "batch," which means two hundred and fifty, and the dealer who owned the mold dispersed them over a six-year period. While I have not seen one of these water pitchers, it doubtless follows in quality all the rest of the Westward-Ho frauds.

The new Rose in Snow goblets were first brought to my attention by Baltimore correspondents. It may have seemed wiser to plant them farther away from Philadelphia, as dealers in that locality had become fake-conscious after the wounds inflicted by the Westward-Ho reproductions. The Rose in Snow goblets were such poor copies that dealers everywhere soon noticed the difference, and warned their customers. As may be noted from the picture on Plate 51 the detail of two tiny leaves is entirely missing, and the new goblets are smaller in size than the old ones. The surface of the original appears to be pebbled, while the fake has such a finely pitted surface that it gives the goblet a frosted look. After the missing detail of the leaves was reported by the writer, the manufacturers inserted them, but did not do it correctly. In the old, this detail stands out, while in the new, the lower of the missing two-part detail clings to the larger leaf below it. Reproduction goblets have been found in clear, blue, yellow, and amber.

Illustrated on Plate 52 is the reproduction Rose in Snow plate, beside an old one. It is not possible to show in a picture the differences in minor details between the old and the new, which may be noted only on close examination. The reproduction is thinner; the casting is poor and the width of the handle is narrower. The most noticeable variation is in the stippling. On the old, the background is as coarse as if it had been coated with fine sand, which gives it a "pebbled" look, though it is a very fine pebbling, to be sure. On the copy, the background, instead of showing the heavily frosted impression, suggests rather melting snow. In brief, it is a thinner stippling, lacking the deeply frosted appearance. New Rose in Snow plates have been circulated in not only clear but blue, amber, and yellow. A Rose in Snow cruet with white overlay has also been reproduced.*

New copies of Moon and Star goblets have been widely circulated. The first batch of goblets came out about 1937. They were much better copies than those I have seen lately. In comparing an old and a new one (of the first batch) I discovered that the narrow band of ribbing which forms a scallop above the "moon," just below the clear band about the upper part of the bowl, was soft to the point of being almost blurred. In the old example, this pressed "cutting" was sharp. The counterfeiters immediately remedied the fault on subsequent runs. Aside from this easily detected difference in the band, the first copy was excellent. The glass was heavy, with the familiar glossy, brilliant surface associated with Moon and Star.

Early in 1945, a collector from the South sent me four pieces of Moon and Star, including a celery vase, eggcup, footed sauce dish, and a goblet. Other collectors wrote me that these much-sought-after pieces had suddenly become common, and certain dealers had been able to furnish any number desired. This fact should sound a danger signal to any collector, whether seasoned or a novice.

The latest Moon and Star reproduction goblet is very poor. To begin with, it has a distinctly greenish tint. The surface is dull instead of glossy. The narrow band of ribbing above the moon has been sharply cut to correct the first error. All goblets were finished by hand, so they can vary in height and width and still be old, but the top of this latest reproduction is so narrow that it would catch the eye of any new collector. No old Moon and Star goblet measures as little as two and five-eighths inches over-all width. From the illustration, one can observe how much narrower it is than the average goblet. The old ones measure close to three inches in diameter. Plate 53. On Plate 54 may be seen a goblet from the first batch of frauds.

The latest copies of the Moon and Star sauce dish and eggcup are much lighter in weight than the originals. The eggcup in particular is so light and so obviously new that it should deceive

---

* Fake mugs have just appeared. See list at end of chapter.

Plate 51

REPRODUCTION ROSE IN SNOW GOBLET IS ON THE RIGHT.

Plate 52

REPRODUCTION ROSE IN SNOW PLATE IS ON THE RIGHT.

Plate 53
MOON IN STAR COUNTERFEITS

Plate 54

REPRODUCTION CHERRY, DAISY AND BUTTON, AND MOON AND STAR GOBLETS.

Plate 55

no one. In a list of glassware and novelties sent out by one of those people who neglect to say whether the merchandise is old or new (it is generally all new), I find the Moon and Star sauce dishes listed at $1.25 each; the goblets at $1.75 each; and the egg-cups omitted altogether. Since the latter represent the greatest rarity, in all probability the producer is out of stock or else the mold is controlled by someone who would not sell to the mail-order house. The celery vase has not been reproduced as far as I know, but unfortunately, the rare water pitcher has been out since shortly after the end of World War II. A list of all the new pieces will be found at the end of this chapter.

A reproduction of the New England Pineapple goblet appeared late in 1937. It is such an excellent copy that it is the glass itself which must be chiefly considered. It not only lacks the bell tone, but plainly shows the difference in the metal. The saw-tooth part of the design is also too sharp. Wine glasses have also been found in general circulation. Plate 55.

Hobnail reproductions have been on the market for years. I believe many of the first copies were made in Czechoslovakia, since so many have been handled by New York importing houses. Glance at the pictures of the new ware which has been selling for over twenty years and observe how different it is from the old forms. Plates 56, 57, 58. Vases have always been a favorite of importers and there are more of them in Hobnail than in any other pattern. Apparently the old technique in making this particular pattern has changed with the passing of time because the hobnails are not at all like the old ones. They are always too blunt and spaced too far apart, or they are hollow, as the old ones seldom were, or else they are slightly elongated and blurred, especially toward the upper part of the new items. Those minus these glaring faults are of a shape unlike any of the old ones. There is not one item on Plate 57 which matches an old specimen, excepting, perhaps, the perfume bottle. No old American Hobnail sugar bowls, jars or vases, were made like those on Plate 58. The square-mouthed water pitcher in that illustration is the best piece, but the hobnails are not right.

Some years ago,* a Philadelphia department store had on sale a beautiful set of opal Hobnail glass. It was not a true reproduction, since none of it was ever made in old glass. A dealer from the West sold me two of the very same goblets. I thought I had found something new. I learned later that that was exactly what I had found! There was everything in that table set—goblets, wines, tumblers, plates in two sizes with scalloped edges, etc. I have never seen any of it since in any shop, so the line may have been discontinued. The goblet is shown on Plate 59.

At one time, rose-opalescent Hobnail became extremely popular, particularly in the Midwest, where it brought higher prices than in the East. Accordingly, new rose-opalescent counterfeits appeared, principally in the form of square-mouthed water pitchers, cream pitchers (several styles and sizes), tumblers and barber bottles. These reproductions were all so poor that they should not have misled any experienced dealer or collector. The hobnails were badly distorted in shape (usually more oval than round) and the rows were too far apart. The square necks on most of the pitchers were almost twice as long as on the old ones. The new cream pitchers were thick, overly heavy and clumsy. Barber bottles were much larger than any of the genuine, not to mention other discrepancies. Plate 60.

Later, a fresh batch of reproductions appeared which differed from those in the first lot. Pictured are four of these new pieces which were shipped in to me, from the state of Oregon, for examination. The dealer, who purchased them in good faith, became suspicious when she found they did not compare favorably with old pieces in her private collection. Plate 61.

The counterfeiters go from one extreme to the other. When they found the earlier Hobnail copies with short, badly distorted hobs were so easily spotted by collectors and dealers, they produced a later lot, which had long, sharp-pointed spinelike hobnails. Instead of being too short or badly formed, they made them too long —too perfect.

The new bell-shaped barber bottle on the left in the illustration

* About 1933.

on Plate 61 is six and three-quarters inches high. In some respects, it is the best copy yet. While the best of the old Hobnail glass had sharp-pointed hobnails, at the same time the old hobs or "warts," as the old glassmakers termed them, were more round at the base, and did not taper outward to such long points. The glass in some of these new bottles has a wavy appearance, not unlike certain silks. In other words, a few of them appear to have a slight film on the outer surface. The pontil is a good semblance of such a mark, but many of the bottles have opaque wavy lines which show up through the base. To return to the Hobnails, the fourth row (beginning with the first ring around the neck and then counting downward) will be noted as pointing slightly upward, whereas in other rows some point straight outward and some upward. Also, some of the rows are closer together than others. In the old bottles, the hobnails are more evenly distributed and none point so decidedly upward.

The usual type of old barber bottle known to collectors is like that with the rounded or bulbous body, which you see illustrated, to the left, on Plate 62. The old Hobnail bottles have a round bowl and a longer neck, with three or four circles of small hobs about it. The average over-all height is from seven and one-quarter inches to seven and three-quarters inches. It is difficult to find them in perfect condition as they underwent hard usage. Often a hob or two, if not more, will be found chipped.

If you look carefully at the illustration of the new barber bottle with the rounded bowl, on Plate 61, you will notice how short and squatty it appears. This is because the neck is shorter and the four rows of hobnails encircling it are closer together. Most of the necks in the old bottles, though not all, measure about four and one-quarter inches long; on the new, about three and one-half inches, so there is quite a difference. This is not an infallible test, as some of the necks on old bottles vary. I have seen genuine ones not over three and one-quarter inches long, but in such a case there were only three rings around the neck and they were far apart. As a whole, I should say the hobnails are longer and thicker on the new bottles. In the smaller bottle, illustrated in the upper row, the hobnails are not quite so long as on the bell-shaped one and they melt away to mere flat dots at the base. I have never seen this in originals. The base has a ground-out pontil, aged by file marks. The base of the bell-shaped bottle bears no sign of age.

The larger cruet pictured, to the right, on Plate 61, appears to have been made by the same company which produced the bell-shaped barber bottle, as the hobnails are the same type—long and spinelike. This cruet is clear blue in the center, shading to opalescent at the top and base. The handle is of clear crystal. Notice how very thick the lip is, compared with the cruet next to it. This cruet has no appearance of age. Moreover, to an experienced buyer it is too heavy in weight, a common failing in reproductions. The hobnails seem too large for the body. There is a faint sign of a pontil mark in the base. These new cruets usually average from five to five and one-quarter inches in height.

The rose-opalescent cruet with the plain crystal handle on the left in the illustration may have been produced by the same company which has been making some of the small cream pitchers. These cream pitchers have been better-than-average copies, with carefully ground-out pontils. You will always notice that they are extremely heavy for their size, and the lips are usually much too thick. In the case of the smaller cruet illustrated, the lip happens to be well made, but the hobnails are so small and flat that they are scarcely more than opalescent spots.

There can be no hard-and-fast rule for detecting spurious Hobnail glass instantly, because so many different factories have been producing it both here and abroad, over a period of years, with the consequent wide variation in forms and types. Of course, it is possible to distinguish the old from the new, but in doing so, consideration must be given to the various types of frauds.

For example, a footed sauce dish in opal Hobnail is pictured on Plate 63 which is obviously a modern piece, since there is no corresponding dish in the old. All genuine Hobnail sauce dishes, even though they vary as to shape, are flat and not footed. Goblets and other matching pieces may also be found. In the same illustration, an example of a large, round Hobnail salt in vivid blue is

Plate 56

HOBNAIL VASES ON THE MARKET FOR THE PAST TWENTY-FIVE YEARS.

Plate 57

HOBNAIL TYPES NEVER MADE IN OLD GLASS.

Plate 58
HOBNAIL REPRODUCTIONS ON THE MARKET FOR YEARS.

MODERN OPAL FRUIT GOBLET.

MODERN OPALESCENT HOBNAIL GOBLET.

Plate 59

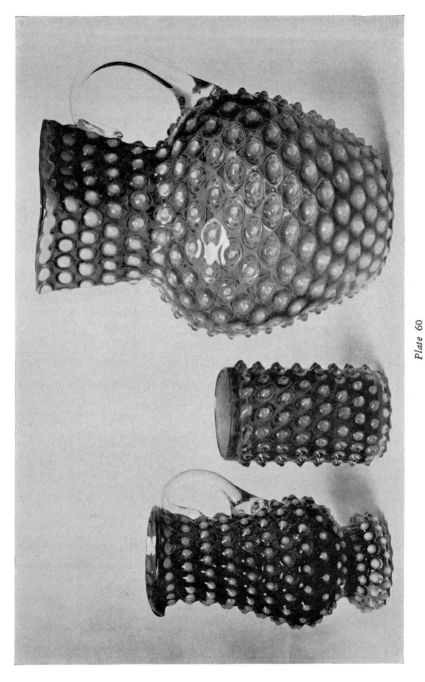

Plate 60

ROSE-OPALESCENT HOBNAIL FROM CZECHOSLOVAKIA.

Plate 61

HOBNAIL REPRODUCTIONS.

Plate 62

OLD AND NEW BARBER BOTTLES. AN ORIGINAL IS ON THE LEFT.

Plate 63

NEW HOBNAIL SAUCE DISH AND SALT. NOVELTY HAT IN CASE GLASS.
MODERN THUMBPRINT GOBLET.

Plate 64

NOVELTY SUGAR AND CREAMER SIMULATING A PUMP AND TROUGH,
THE OLD ARE ON THE LEFT.

presented. Many of these have found their way into antique shops and exhibits.

Some time ago, in one of New England's most famous eating places, which has a small gift department, I was startled to see Puss-in-boots slippers in Hobnail. They were never made in this pattern originally. These slippers were displayed in opal, blue, and in yellow. Other new gift items were small Hobnail fan-shaped trays in the same colors as the slippers. In fact, after viewing the gift shops, one must conclude that the Hobnail and Daisy and Button patterns are in the most favor—at least for the time being.

As most collectors and dealers realize, the Hobnail trough-shaped dish illustrated on Plate 64, is a late Victorian piece, which was made in crystal with opalescent coloring, in yellow, blue, green or amber; also, with opalescent touches. It apparently was meant for sugar, to be paired with the pump creamer shown with it. They are relatively unimportant and do not sell for enough to justify any manufacturer in copying them. The one at the left in the photograph is old, and is placed so that the detail of the cob-web design that simulates the lines of growth apparent in any log cross section, may be plainly seen. In the originals, the cobweb is complete and shows fine detail. In the new, the web is loosely constructed, with little detail. On the ends of the four feet in the old dish, there are several concentric circles. In the new, there is barely one crude circle. Again, the old has a fairly large hobnail on the inside of each foot which is lacking in the new, though there is an evident attempt at making a slight hump. There are fewer hobnails on the new dish and they are spaced differently from the old. Altogether, there are enough points of difference so that no one should be deluded into buying a new one, if a normal amount of care and discretion are used by the purchaser.

Illustrated with the trough is the glass pump, that has also been copied. An original specimen of this is shown at the left. It is in a clear turquoise-blue glass, with a blue-opalescent coloring in the scalloped top. The copy, at the right, clearly shows several differences, even at first glance. The old piece has a scalloped top and the new a plain edge. The copy also has an opalescent tinge in the handle, in the spigot and over three-quarters of the container. There are other points of dissimilarity which may not be easily observed in the illustration. For instance, the surface of the old vase is clear and soft to the touch, whereas the glass in the new one is not only cloudy but the surface is rough, particularly on the inside. Another point that may be noted with many such reproductions is that the edges are invariably thicker.

There are more reproductions today in the Daisy and Button pattern than in any other single design. It would almost seem to be enjoying a wider sale now than it did originally. Goblets appeared in the early 1930's, in clear and in colors. One style was made which is not a copy of any known old one. It has a clear panel on each end and a flat stem, carrying a design similar to that on the bowl. Vases and other pieces came out to match. The goblet is illustrated on Plate 65 and a vase on Plate 66.

Plates were next on the list, the first being the seven-inch square one, in clear and in colors. In due course of time, there were seven- and ten-inch round ones, in clear and in colors, with a scalloped edge.

Hats and slippers were soon on the market, in various sizes and colors. There is no hard-and-fast rule regarding reproduction Daisy and Button hats because the new ones have been turned out by several different factories, with variations in detail. Most of the new ones are too heavy, the edge of the brim is too thick, the buttons are sharp rather than softly molded and with a glossy surface, as they almost invariably should be. Moreover, practically *all* the new Daisy and Button glass, no matter what the form, has one common failing. When held to the light, the clear portions of the design reveal what I can only describe as a "crinkly" appearance. It should all be perfectly clear and usually, though perhaps not always, with a glossiness on the buttons. This "crinkly" appearance in the glass may be found on practically all pieces from a ten-inch plate to a two-inch slipper. Sometimes the clear portion is merely noticeably dull, instead of crinkly. The shades of color in the new Daisy and Button also vary from the old, being harsher and deeper. The old are almost invariably soft and mellow in tone. Plate 66.

During the 1930's, a round Daisy and Button plate, unlike any old one, was offered by certain wholesalers. The border is divided by three panels, and the center is rayed, with a flower ornament. Plate 68. Such pieces add to the general confusion of old and new. A subsequent arrival was a six-inch round plate, with a scallop and point edge. It was well distributed in California.

Novelties in Daisy and Button, unknown among original old items, are frequently seen on sale in ten-cent stores. A gypsy kettle on three feet with its edges adapted to hold cigarettes is one addition. Also, two styles of matchholders, with or without handles. Such oddities do less harm because they are too obviously modern.

One last note of caution regarding Daisy and Button hats: Genuine hats in emerald-green or ruby-red are unknown. Old hats may be found in unusual variations, such as crystal with a red brim, or crystal with the buttons in red or blue. Yellow-opalescent and blue-opalescent constitute rarities in this group.

The shoes on roller skates illustrated on Plates 76 and 86, were purchased from a wholesale house for 50¢ each. They are in blue and in clear; others have appeared in a number of colors. The upper part is in a fine cube pattern, and the shoe portion has a mottled effect, as if in imitation of alligator leather. There is an old shoe, similar but slightly larger, with the edge scalloped instead of plain. Apparently the reproduction is copied from it, with slight variations.

Modern Ivy in Snow was seen during the 1930's both in clear glass and in milk-white. Originally the set was made in "crystal" (old term for "clear") with an occasional piece, such as a celery vase, to be found in milk-white. The stippled background of the new glass is so thin that the glass lacks the finely pebbled appearance of the old. Plate 55. It is claimed some of the Ivy in Snow pieces, if not all of them, are made from original molds. If so, the molds must have undergone some recutting or else became badly worn over the years, because it is possible to tell the old from the new glass by the appearance of the surface. To the best of my

Plate 65

MODERN FORMS IN A HOBNAIL GOBLET, AND DAISY AND BUTTON.
IN THE CENTER IS A NEW "LACY SANDWICH."

DAISY AND BUTTON FAKES.   COPIES OF HAND VASES.

Plate 67
DAISY AND BUTTON PLATE AND DEEP DESSERT DISH.
TWO SIZES IN NEW DAISY AND BUTTON SLIPPERS,
AND A BABY SHOE IN MARBLE GLASS.

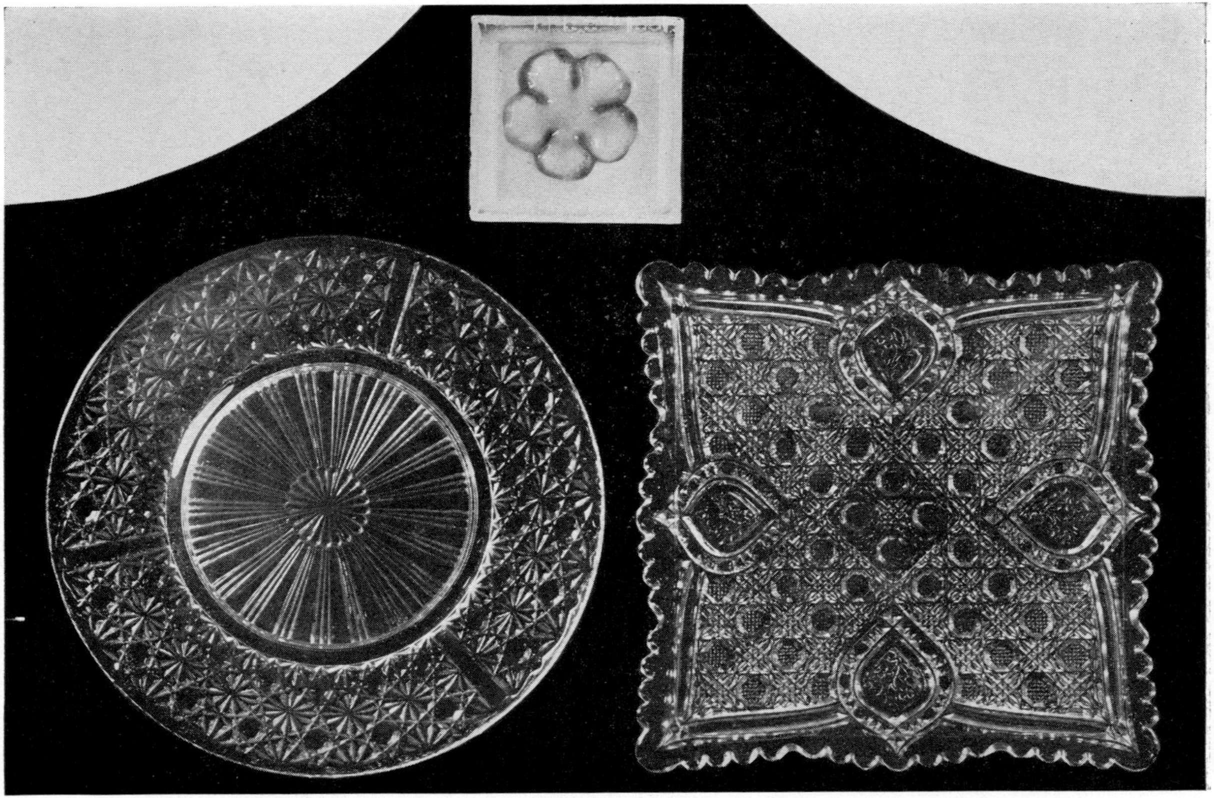

Plate 68

MODERN PLATES IN SPRAY AND CANE, AND DAISY AND BUTTON.

Plate 69

REPRODUCTION DAISY AND BUTTON GOBLETS AND CHAMPAGNES.
NEW HAND VASE.

COPY OF EARLY BLOWN GOBLET

FAKE DAISY AND BUTTON GOBLET

Plate 70

knowledge, no original pattern glass molds exist that would be very much over fifty years old. Moreover, they will not stand considerable usage because they not only become worn, but they sometimes break. Original iron molds are big, heavy, clumsy things, and as the officer of one old glass company told me, they took up too much room to store and so as patterns went out of style, they were melted up for scrap and the metal used over again. Those that have lasted are very likely no older, to be generous, than the 1890's. Apparently some do exist for such patterns as Ivy in Snow and Lace Dewdrop, but so many false claims have been put forth as to the use of genuine old molds for other items, such as cup plates, that the reader would be well advised to disregard most of them. Moreover, any collector should be properly skeptical of the type of antique dealer who claims his glass is not reproduction but *"continuation"* glass. By this, the dealer means the glass cannot be termed new since it has come from old molds! In nine cases out of ten, the "continuation" glass does not emanate from original molds. It is reproduction. The reader can decide whether he considers recent glass made from molds fifty to sixty years old, modern or not. The only apparently reliable claims I have heard to old pattern glass molds are for Ivy in Snow, Lace Dewdrop, and a Moon and Star variant. The Blackberry which I have seen in department stores *may* also be from old molds, but it bears no relation to the older milk-white Blackberry shown in *Early American Pressed Glass*. Reproductions of goblets and a creamer in the earlier pattern have been out for some time. The newer so-called Blackberry has a long stem with some leaves, and berries which more closely resemble a small cluster of grapes. There is a single berry from each long stem. Differences between the quality of old and new milk-white glass will be discussed in Chapter VII, devoted to that ware.

Lace Dewdrop, a pattern which was made originally by George Duncan & Sons of Pittsburgh, Pa., and continued later by the Co-operative Flint Glass Company of Beaver Falls, Pa., is claimed to be carried on from old molds. It was one of Duncan's later patterns and since this concern is still operating, it is curious that they should have disposed of the molds. It is said that in the 1920's the molds were again sold, the Phoenix Glass Company of Monica, Pa., being the next purchaser. They supposedly put out some of the pattern in clear glass. For some reason, they decided not to continue this pattern, possibly because the popularity of pressed tableware was at a low ebb then. So the molds were again sold to a glass jobber, who rented them out for a time, but finally sold them to an Ohio glass manufacturer. It is now being made in quantity, in milk-white. Plate 96.

An old and a new Blackbery goblet are shown here, the reproduction being at the right. The photographer remarked, when he was taking this picture, that even he did not need to be told which was the copy! Plate 71.

In producing this type of glass, the original intent of the manufacturer was to copy china or porcelain at a lesser cost and, therefore, the Blackberry pattern was referred to in their patent as "hot-caste porcelain." The desired effect was a dense white. When certain ingredients of the batch burned out, as sometimes happened, the workmen said it had "gone flinty"—meaning the glass showed opaline tints instead of being a dead-white. This rarely occurred in the Blackbery pattern, though often it is found with dirty streaks, occurring at the foot of the goblets.

The new Blackberry goblet is not made of a dense white glass. Neither is it opalescent. It has more of a "pearly" white appearance. The design is badly blurred, instead of standing out in clear, heavy relief as it always does in the old pieces. There is a translucent edge around the foot of some of the new goblets, which shows clearly in the illustration. This might not occur in all the copies, so students should not rely on this point as an infallible test. The quality of the design tells the story. Later on, the mold for the goblet was apparently recut, as the later copies are somewhat superior to the first. I have not seen the new creamers, but they doubtless may be told by the quality and coloring of the milk-white, as well as by discrepancies in the detail.

As far back as 1939, we learned that Lion goblets and sauce

dishes had been reproduced. From time to time, rumors reached me that other pieces in the Lion pattern had been copied. So many false alarms are circulated that in most cases I can do no more than offer warnings, until I obtain conclusive proof of the counterfeits. In 1940, a shipment of Lion glass came in to me from a dealer to examine. She felt the pieces did not look right. Her suspicions were well founded.

Pictured on Plate 72 is an old Lion oval compote base between a new sugar bowl and a new spoon holder. As is usually the case, the differences between old and new are much more easily distinguishable, placed side by side. In the old compote base, the design is as clearly defined as the details in a finely carved cameo. The lion stands out in higher relief, particularly the hip. All of the detail work on the lion displays the evidence of finer workmanship. In the new, the detail is better in the cover than in the base. The design is softer, the detail is somewhat blurred, though the effect as a whole is good until studied closely. It is difficult to describe the curious difference between the old and new frosted backgrounds. Every frosted and clear combination is first produced in all-crystal glass; the frosted section is created by dipping the portion to be so finished in what old glassmakers used to term "white acid." Most of the old frosted or "satin" finish is a grayish-white. The softer appearance of the new Lion pieces is doubtless due to the poor modeling, which is in lower relief; for certainly the old has a distinctive clarity of detail and background not found in the new.

Also pictured are two new Lion celery vases. One is distinctly yellowish, like the first batch of new Westward-Ho goblets that came out in 1936; the second is too dead a white. The modeling in the stems and bases is much like that found in the new Lion, Westward-Ho and Three Face goblets. Plate 73.

These copies were originally planted largely in Maryland (particularly Baltimore), Ohio and Indiana. They were not in evidence in New England, even at the antique shows, where dealers congregate from all sections. Following the appearance of the medium-sized, oval covered compotes, covered sugar bowls, celery vases, and spoon holders, there came the creamers and butter dishes, large round bread plate and eggcups.

Illustrated on Plate 74 is an old and a new Lion sauce dish. The genuine one is at the left. Again the differences are plainly discernible when the two are side by side, though it must be admitted that the reproductions might deceive many an unwary buyer. In the case of the original and new Three Face pieces, the glass of the *old* appears *alive,* whereas that of the new looks dead and the frosted finish is chalklike. The same holds true of the Lion sauce dishes. In the old, the detail is in sharp relief, particularly the lion's head, the mane, and the minute detail of the hairs of the body. Also the finish is a gray-white. In the illustration, notice the difference in the color of the frosted part. The reproduction is much whiter, and the workmanship is coarse and more uneven.

The newest fraud to come to my attention is an eight-inch, round, covered Lion compote, with rampant lion knob. Possibly because I have studied so many reproductions, I recognized it as a copy almost on sight. In this compote, the frosting is harsh to the touch; the detail of the pattern is quite poor, especially in the lion's face; and the glass itself looks new. As for the Lion goblets, while there are discrepancies in detail, the easiest way to tell the new ones is in the lion's mouth. It is a straight line on all three faces, in the old, and the lion has a pleasant expression. In the new, the line of the lip appears about the same on two, but is twisted down on the third, thus giving the lion a rather mean, ugly appearance. The set of the lion's mouth is a sure test of his age. Plate 75.

Some time ago, a glass manufacturer in this country displayed a set of glassware under the name of the Thousand Eye pattern. It differed so much from the old design that it could do no possible harm beyond causing false rumors to spread regarding the reproduction of an old pattern. But a copy of the old Thousand Eye goblet has been circulated since then which is clever enough to deceive any careless buyer. Therefore, everyone interested in these goblets would do well to study them thoroughly. The clear glass,

Plate 71

OLD AND NEW SPANISH LACE TUMBLERS, AND MILK-WHITE
BLACKBERRY GOBLETS. THE FAKES ARE ON THE RIGHT.

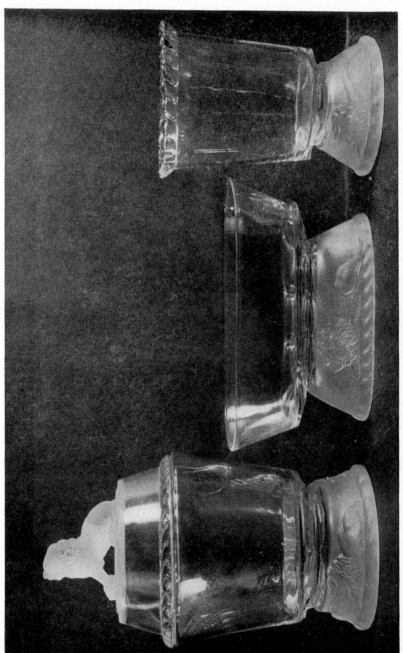

Plate 72
LION PATTERN.

Plate 73
TWO NEW LION CELERY VASES.

Plate 74

OLD AND NEW LION SAUCE DISH. THE FAKE IS ON THE RIGHT.

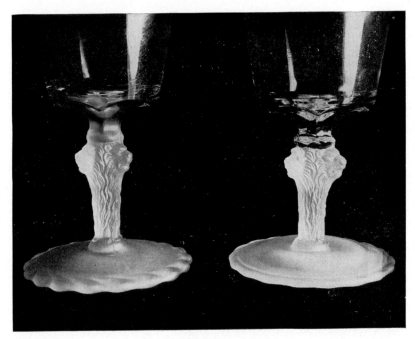

Plate 75
THE REPRODUCTION LION GOBLET IS ON THE RIGHT.

or lighter colored, goblet pictured on Plate 76 is the latest counterfeit. Perceptible differences may be noted, even in the photograph. The old goblet is more graceful, and the mold was executed by a better workman. The bowl is more flaring; the "eyes" are deeper set and more rounded, and the points between the eyes are a trifle larger and more outstanding. The stem is longer and more graceful on the old and the knob is smaller. In fact, the simplest method of differentiating an old goblet from a new one is in the length of the stem. The old ones measured two and five-eighths inches from the base of the bowl to the bottom of the foot. Hold the goblet in your hand, sideways, in measuring. The reproductions measure a trifle over two and three-eighths inches, or a very scant two and one-half inches. Another noticeable difference is in the edge directly above the uppermost row or eyes. In the old, it is distinctly indented, with a very decided arch. In the new, this edge is scarcely indented at all, so the arch is hardly noticeable. If collectors and dealers will take the time to study these obvious differences in the counterfeits, there will be no reason for anyone to be sorry. The reproductions I have seen were in clear, amber, yellow and blue. Plates in the eight-inch size followed, in the same color range.

New Shell and Tassel goblets made their appearance about 1940. In the accompanying illustration on Plate 77, the old goblet is at the right. No picture could show the one point of difference by which it is comparatively easy to detect the counterfeit. Between the large shell ornaments which adorn the bowl is a small conventional motif which has a clear space in the center. By holding an old goblet to the light and looking directly through this space, it will be found to be absolutely clear. In the new goblet, if examined as closely, the reaction after looking through the space is that the glass is wavy. This is difficult to describe but easy to understand, after comparing an old goblet with a new one. It was not a complicated pattern to copy, and thus the workmanship of the counterfeit is fairly accurate.

In describing the glass as "wavy" in the copy, I do not mean that there are actually wrinkles or that the glass is cloudy, but the difference is much the same as it would be between looking out of a fine freshly washed window and another in which the glass was defective, thereby blurring the clearness of the vision.

New copies of the Diamond Cut with Leaf goblets and wine glasses are out. I do not have an original goblet of this pattern for illustrative purposes; but, at first glance, it will be perfectly apparent that the new goblets are much lighter in weight than the old. Their newness should not confuse anyone except a novice. The same holds true of the wine glasses. The old is not only much heavier in weight, but the stem and foot are considerably thicker. I noted that the foot of the new goblet is thin and small. Old Diamond Cut with Leaf goblets often vary, particularly in height and in the quality of the glass, but the counterfeits will be found to be uniformly new and alike in weight, height, and appearance.

Pictured on Plate 78 are three new goblets which have been mentioned before as a warning to collectors, but not illustrated. That on the left is in the Paneled Thistle pattern. It is a late midwestern design in imitation of cut glass, but has been in favor with some collectors in recent years. The goblet was made originally in two forms: one has a straight-sided bowl, the other has a flaring brim as shown in the picture. This would not be a difficult mold to copy, but I think it is quite likely an old one was found and utilized, since this design was not first made before the 1890's. The only way to tell an old Paneled Thistle goblet from a new one would be by the appearance of the glass. The new ones look new. Old ones have had some years of usage, and the wear removes a slight amount of the surface gloss. If any dealer or collector contemplates the purchase of any of these goblets, about which there is any suspicion, it would be wiser to be safe rather than sorry, and pass them by. So far as I know, Paneled Thistle goblets with the straight-sided bowls have not been copied. It is the type pictured here which needs to be examined with care. Paneled Thistle salts followed, as well as plates, in the seven-, nine-, and ten-inch sizes.

Pleat and Panel goblets were made in two forms originally, one as illustrated on Plate 78 with the panels or bars protruding above the design, and the other type with the projecting panels on a level with the rest of the design. Only the style shown here has been copied. On comparing an old goblet with a new one, I found the foot or base of the new to be smaller, as may be noted in the picture. In the reproductions, the stippled stripes on the stems of some are crooked, and, in others, it may be noted that the stripes are wider and thicker. There is also a distinct difference in the stippling in the "window" or panel, on the goblet bowl. On most of the counterfeits, the stippling is much lighter and not so evenly distributed. The panel itself stands out like a windowpane, with a higher edge to the panel. A Pleat and Panel seven-inch plate has also been reproduced, and the same faulty stippling applies to it.

In the Paneled Grape, practically whole new sets have been marketed since the 1930's. There is probably more of this vintage

Grape pattern about today, than there is in the original. Of course the old is not particularly ancient. It was made in Indiana, as far as it has been possible to learn, and probably dates in the 1890's. The quality of the original glass varied considerably, some of it having a glossy, clear surface and others being dull, yellowish or merely evidencing a poor, cheap quality of metal. The reproductions are much more apt to display an evenness of whiteness and quality. In the original design, the grape leaves were in heavy relief and well covered with stippling. In the new, there is almost no stippling. This difference shows prominently when old and new pieces are placed side by side. The tumbler in the center of Plate 79 is genuine. There was a time when we depended on differences in the detail of the design on the goblets to tell the story but apparently more than one, if not several, goblet molds have been utilized, so a surer key is in the stippling of the leaves. Plate 79.

Reproductions in the Three Face pattern also came out during the 1930's. As happened in the Westward-Ho, goblets and sauce dishes appeared first. Many of the earliest goblets were harsh to the touch, on the frosted part of the foot. This is not always a reliable index today because some of the later copies are smoother and softer. However, any pieces that feel harsh instead of soft, should be viewed with suspicion. The frosting on the new is always too white and the detail is not as fine, especially in the shape of the noses. When an old Three Face goblet is held to a strong light, the finely chiseled features of the gray-white face appear to have life. The dead-white and lifeless appearance of the new face may be detected more readily under a bright electric light. When the photographer's powerful floodlights hit the faces pictured on Plate 80, no one would have the slightest difficulty in telling the new from the old. In the reproduction four and one-half-inch sauce dish, the faces are even poorer than on the goblets. Also, on some of these dishes the saucer part is thicker and sometimes turns in somewhat at the top.

The covered six-inch butter dish came next, though this is usually listed by dealers selling the copies, as a compote. All three styles of champagnes have also been copied and marketed since before World War II. The last known fake in this pattern is the lamp, which has a scalloped foot and rounded, clear bowl.

Bakewell, Pears & Company of Pittsburgh, Pa., produced during the 1860's a pattern known today simply as Ribbon. Some dealers and collectors refer to it as "early Ribbon" to differentiate it from later varieties. This glass has one frosted panel alternating with a clear indented panel.

Among the reproductions put out by one glass company is a copy of the Ribbon goblet. The new one is taller and slightly heavier than the original. The frosted panel on the old Ribbon pattern was accomplished by sandblasting, a process which antedated the use of acid as a method of applying a frosted finish. "White acid," as the glassmakers termed it, leaves a soft, rose-petal surface while sandblasting leaves the surface smooth but with a firm, coarser feel to it. I do not know how the present-day sandblasting is achieved, but the panels on the new Ribbon goblet are harsh and rough to the touch, and some of the panels show faintly diagonal lines, as if scratched or filed. Moreover, the frosting is whiter on the new goblet, as is usually the case. Weighing glass, as a method of detecting frauds, may offer distinct possibilities, since the new is invariably heavier. An old and a new Ribbon goblet are pictured on Plate 81.

Copies of the Tulip wines have been out since about 1940. When an old and a new one are placed side by side, one wonders how anybody could be taken in by the frauds. They are shown on Plate 82. The old is much thicker and heavier, the knob in the stem is much larger and the foot is larger and thicker. The differences may be plainly seen in the illustration.

Beaded Grape goblets and large square plates, in emerald green and in clear glass, appeared on the market after the close of World War II. The goblet seems to be a good copy until placed alongside an old one. However, there are the usual discrepancies in detail. The easiest method of detecting the fraud is to examine the cluster of grapes hanging from the upper bough at the left, which is plainly visible in the illustration on Plate 82. This cluster hangs on an exceedingly short stem in the old, which is at the right. The stem is a good quarter of an inch long on the copy.

Reproductions of Baltimore Pear goblets, plates, sugar bowls and sauce dishes have been distributed since the late 1930's. The simplest way to detect the fake is in the detail that forms the background of the leaves. Notice the wavy, loose lines in the new one on Plate 83, as against the vast amount of fine lines on the old, which create a network for the heavier veins that stand out in higher relief. This network of fine lines when studied closely, presents an exquisite appearance on the sauce dish, and is a compliment to the moldworker responsible for the excellent workmanship displayed.

Emerald green Herringbone goblets (Plate 164, No. 1—*Early American Pressed Glass*) came out along about 1948. They have also been made in clear glass. The green goblets do not have the depth of color of the old, and the glass itself looks new. The original green Herringbone is a fine deep shade of emerald green. The goblets and plates have always been scarce, hence the frauds. Sauce dishes and berry bowls are relatively common, so dealers and collectors should have little difficulty in telling the new goblets since all that is necessary is to compare the shade of color with an old sauce dish or bowl.

Just one item has been reproduced in the popular Frosted Coin pattern at present and that is the toothpick holder. These have been on the market for some time. The reproduction is much heavier than the old, the frosting is poor and the coins extend down into the curved arc of the base. The figures on the coin are not sharp and distinct, and the word "Liberty" is so poorly copied as to be scarcely legible. Also, the "hair-do" and head ornaments, as well as the face, are blurred. The stars are larger than on the old. Altogether, it should not be difficult for collectors of Frosted Coin to spot the new toothpick holders.

A popular goblet among collectors is known as Strawberry and Currant. So far as it has been possible to ascertain, the originals were never made in color. Copies have been out in clear, amber, blue, and yellow since about 1945. By and large, the new ones are

Plate 76

OLD AND NEW THOUSAND EYE GOBLETS. THE FAKE IS ON THE RIGHT.
REPRODUCTION HOBNAIL CREAMER, AND A SHOE.

Plate 77
OLD AND NEW SHELL AND TASSEL GOBLET.
THE COPY IS ON THE RIGHT.

Plate 78

REPRODUCTION PANELED THISTLE, CHERRY, AND PLEAT AND PANEL GOBLETS.

Plate 79

Upper Row: REPRODUCTION INVERTED THUMBPRINT TUMBLER AND FINGER BOWL.
THE OLD TUMBLER IS IN THE CENTER.

Lower Row: THREE PANELED GRAPE TUMBLERS.
THE ONE IN THE CENTER IS OLD, THE OTHERS ARE NEW

Plate 80
ENLARGED DETAIL IN OLD AND NEW THREE FACE GOBLETS.
THE ONE ON THE LEFT IS OLD.

Plate 81

OLD AND NEW RIBBON GOBLETS. THE FAKE IS ON THE RIGHT.
THREE COPIES OF CRANBERRY INVERTED THUMBPRINT.

Plate 82

REPRODUCTION AND OLD TULIP WINES, AND BEADED GRAPE GOBLETS.
THE FAKES ARE ON THE RIGHT.

Plate 83
OLD AND NEW BALTIMORE PEAR GOBLET.
THE FAKE IS ON THE RIGHT.

Plate 84
OLD AND NEW STRAWBERRY AND CURRANT GOBLET.
THE COPY IS ON THE RIGHT, REVERSED.
REPRODUCTION FROSTED CIRCLE AND ROMAN ROSETTE GOBLETS.

better than average reproductions. The foot is as thick as it should be. The detail of the design makes a good appearance until placed alongside an old one. On close inspection quite a difference will be noted in the arrangement of the currants, and the shape and detail in the leaves are much finer in the old, as is to be expected. The strawberries are crude, and considerable detail is lacking in the copies. This may be noted in the illustration on Plate 84.

The Crystal Wedding is a late pattern which was originated by Adams & Company of Pittsburgh. It was carried on later by the United States Glass Company, also of Pittsburgh, after they absorbed seventeen of the older glass firms from in and near Pittsburgh, about 1893. Illustrated on Plate 85 are an old and a new compote, the original being at the left. Apparently a new mold was made, since there are numerous discrepancies in the design. The contours of the steps leading to the knob on the cover are sharper in the old. Again, the almond-pointed thumbprints in the band about the cover are clearly defined and sharp; whereas, in the old, they appear to run together. It may be noted even in the illustration that there is a considerable difference in the almond points around the base of the compote. These also show careless workmanship in the new—being slightly crooked, and as if they had been cut out with a knife. In the old, they are uniformly long, straight ovals. In the step next to this decorated band on the foot may be seen the chief difference in the detail. One will notice that below the clear space in this step, which almost seems to overlap, the edge is scalloped; whereas, in the new, it is left plain. The new compote is somewhat more squat and the square stem is thicker. The simplest way to detect the reproduction is by the non-scalloped space directly above the foot. Altogether, there should be no difficulty for anyone interested in glass in telling the differences between the old and new Crystal Wedding compotes. The new ones have been produced in more than one size! Also, they are found in clear glass, or decorated in red. Many of the copies, when placed beside originals, show a greenish tint in the glass.

Several reproduction goblets have appeared, in which no other

matching pieces have been noted. The Cherry goblet (Plate 66,
Early American Pressed Glass) was out about 1940, or possibly
earlier. In this, the quality of the glass does not match the old,
and the design is sharper. Plate 78. Next to be noticed were the
Roman Rosette and the Frosted Circle goblets. The Roman Rosette
has the same type of thin stippling in the band around the bowl,
as has been mentioned in connection with Rose in Snow. This
stippling should not be so even and thin, giving a frosted look.
It should, instead, be like miniature pebbles. The glass itself looks
new. The foot is too thin. The Frosted Circle is a better copy, as
the glass is heavier and the foot thicker. The difference can be
quickly noted in the frosted circle itself. This is rather crudely
done, some of the circles looking as if they had been ground down
on the sides to make them more flat, before they were frosted.
These two new ones may be seen on Plate 84.

Ruby Thumbprint has been out since 1940, and perhaps longer.
The featured pieces on wholesalers' lists have been goblets, finger
bowls (not made originally) cordials, wines, champagnes, and
three other items not made originally, sherbets (a footed compote
three inches high), a "Highball" (five and a half inch tumbler),
and an "Old Fashion" (tumbler, four inches high). Sometimes
the tumbler appears listed as a fruit juice glass, and the "Highball," as a lemonade glass. "Cocktails" have also been quoted.
This is merely a wine glass which has been made wider and more
flaring at the top. Any of these new pieces may be spotted by
careful buyers because the red coloring has a distinct copper tint
in it. It is known that a ten and one-half inch covered compote has
been on the market, so there may be other forms which I have not
seen or heard about. All of the items noted are made in clear
glass, too. When in clear they are referred to as King's Crown.
Any buyer would do well to examine with care any purchases in
this pattern. Plate 86.

Red Block goblets and wines have been about for some time,
though not nearly as long as the Ruby Thumbprint. Here again
the coloring in the red block should tell the story.

What is advertised today as Thumbprint by some dealers in reproductions does not bear much resemblance to the old pattern, all of which was in flint glass. There are many variants of the Thumbprint pattern, particularly in the goblets, but those which are collectible in complete sets of tableware in the early and desirable glass are illustrated in *Early American Pressed Glass.* The new goblet has a tapering bowl with two rows of elongated thumbprints and carries a double knob stem. Needless to say the reproduction is of the modern "soft" or lime glass. Matching wines and tumblers are also listed. Another modern goblet in imitation of Thumbprint is shown on Plate 63.

A pattern listed as "Daisy" in *Early American Pressed Glass,* somewhat similar to Daisy and Button, has been made in large-size sauce dishes and celery dips since the 1930's. This design was produced during the early 1900's and since it is so late, it is possible that the old molds were found. There has not been enough popular demand for this glass to warrant the expense of making new ones.

Another odd dish which may also be produced from an original mold, is a sauce dish in the shape of a leaf. This is not the better-known Maple Leaf, which rests on three feet.

In the upper row of the illustration on Plate 79 are shown an old and a new cranberry-colored Inverted Thumbprint tumbler and a new finger bowl. The original cranberry tumbler of this pattern is in the center. It is taller, lighter in weight and has smaller thumbprints. In fact, it weighs just a quarter of a pound, though one should not always judge by the weight alone, since the old ones do vary. Even so, the new tumbler, which is much shorter and somewhat larger in diameter, weighs a half pound and has a much larger thumbprint pattern. This copy is so exceedingly heavy for its size that I think most collectors would be suspicious of it. Actually, a great deal of the reproduction Inverted Thumbprint may be detected by the weight, and the size of the thumbprints. They are often much too large.

During the war when iron for molds was too difficult to obtain to continue making new pressed glass fakes, a great many blown glass copies appeared in novelty wares. Among these were such items as the rose-opalescent hat pictured on Plate 87, and many pink, blue, or opal Inverted Thumbprint bowls like the one also illustrated in the upper row. The hats are shown merely to keep the record straight. Old ones of this type and pattern are not known to exist. New bowls may be easily told because all those I have seen in case glass (or that having a white lining) have had a ground-out pontil mark on the base, generally with a dull frosted appearance to it. These bowls in plain colors, without a lining, do not usually carry a pontil scar.

The water pitcher at the right in the lower row of Plate 87 is a reproduction in cranberry red. The pitcher at the left is old. Notice how clumsy and thick the lip is on the copy. The thumb spots are larger and not so graduated in shape on the new one and it is much heavier in weight. The frilled edge is much thicker on the new pieces. New water pitchers may also be found in different shapes. There is one style with a decidedly bulbous body, plain folded edge and crystal spun handle. Creamers to match are found in numerous sizes and colors, including emerald-green.

The popular cruets have been made in cranberry Inverted Thumbprint, with crystal spun handles and crystal stoppers. Often the new stoppers are hexagonal in shape, long and pointed. One of the latest cruets has three rows of thumprints, a tricorn-shaped frilled edge and is heavy in weight.

It is difficult to set hard-and-fast rules to follow in watching the Inverted Thumbprint reproductions because they are blown glass. The companies making these copies may or may not add a pontil mark to pitchers or bowls. In looking over a group of undeniably old water pitchers, I found the only one having a pontil mark was a choice one in amberina. The best test is in the weight, size, and shape of the thumprints, and the thickness of the lip. There are so many forms, colors, and combinations of colors that the reader had best consult the list of new items appended to the end of this chapter. Two additional new tumblers and a pitcher are shown on Plate 81.

Reproductions in Spanish Lace are not difficult to tell from the old. On Plate 71 are pictured an old and a new tumbler. The leaf and flower pattern is so clear and distinct in the old that it almost seems to be enameled. One can feel the design both on the inside and outside of a tumbler. In the new, the pattern is so diffused through the glass that almost no pattern can be felt and the whole effect is more indistinct. The new tumbler actually does not appear quite so bad as it looks in the illustration, due to the fact that there are reflections of the pattern through the glass. The copies seen most frequently are of finger bowls, pitchers, tumblers, cruets, syrup pitchers, and sugar shakers.

A new Thistle goblet is out like the one shown on Plate 140 in *Early American Pressed Glass.* The only copies I have seen bore the trademark of the concern putting them out, embossed directly underneath the stem, in the cupped part of the foot where it would be well-nigh impossible for a grinding wheel to get at it. Such an honest method of marking is a heartening sign. However, on a wholesalers' list there was a "Ruby Thistle goblet." This I have not seen so cannot be sure which Thistle it meant, since there are more than one.

Certain agents selling new glass resorted for a while to a form of deception consisting of offering new goblets under titles that belong to different patterns as they are named in my book, *Early American Pressed Glass.* The new bear so little resemblance to the old that they can do little harm, unless purchased by mail from the type of dealer who will not make good. For instance, a goblet listed as "Fine Rib" is illustrated on Plate 88. Collectors will see at a glance how different it is from that fine, early flint glass to which that designation really belongs. Other brand-new goblets are listed under such names as "Lacy Sandwich," "Icicle," "Waffle," "Thumbprint" and "Inverted Thumbprint" which are not even copies of the originals. Two more of these outlaws are pictured on Plate 88. The one on the right was sent to me as "Waffle." The other matches a modern plate shown on Plate 89.

Many people write to me about the plate shown on Plate 89. By its coarseness it should never mislead any collector into thinking it to be Lacy Sandwich. They were sold in the ten-cent stores in clear, light green and salmon pink. I saw them twenty-five years ago. This pattern was made in complete sets of tableware. Two other plates which are gift shop merchandise are illustrated. Plate 90. I have seen them in antique shops and have received inquiries about them. These are also modern, and were made in clear and in colors.

There is no true old "Lacy Sandwich" set of glass. Advertisements of such "Lacy Sandwich" by department stores as copies of a design produced by the Boston & Sandwich Glass Company on Cape Cod are actually sales talk, the information usually being supplied by the company or agents selling it. No complete set of tableware, all of one lacy pattern, was ever made in the early days when such glass was in vogue. The pattern which now is offered under the trade name of "Lacy Sandwich" by the firm who makes it, merely carries a motif that was employed both by Sandwich and by Baccarat, in France. Indeed, a pattern that resembles it was made by Baccarat until World War II stopped them.

Some years ago, a man in central New York State decided to make reproductions his main business. He himself was not a glass manufacturer, so his orders had to be executed by others. One of the first copies he introduced was of the popular Lacy Sandwich cake plate, in what is known as the Beehive pattern. I could not find a new one to illustrate, so decided to picture a genuine one, as a means of identifying the pattern. This is shown on Plate 91. The old plate in this silvery, lacy glass is of heavy lead-flint glass. The copies are glaringly new.

Quite a large number of pieces after the old Lacy Sandwich Beehive design are about in various shapes, sizes, and colors. Originally nothing was made in that pattern at Sandwich except an octagonal cake plate, fairly deep in the center, measuring nine and one-eighth inches in diameter. Shallow green bowls, six and a half inches in diameter, were on sale for months in Boston shops. Lately I came across a flat golden amber Beehive plate, measuring nine and three-quarters inches, and a deeper plate in amber, more like the original, measuring a scant nine inches. These are the best copies I have seen. Other plates are made in clear and in colors, perhaps by another concern, in an extra-large size as well as a small butter plate. The copies are lighter in weight, and the surfaces very glossy whereas the old glass always possesses a soft dullness, the equivalent of the mellow patina on old furniture. Collectors should experience no trouble in perceiving the difference. Pictured with the old Sandwich plate is a Baccarat plate, from which a modern set of "lacy" glass has been copied.

The square glass plate illustrated on Plate 68 probably dates in the early 1900's. It has been listed frequently on wholesalers' sheets under the name of "Cane and Spray," in peach, amber, yellow, and clear glass. It is pictured here for no other reason

Plate 85
OLD AND NEW CRYSTAL WEDDING COMPOTES.
THE REPRODUCTION IS ON THE RIGHT.

Plate 86

OLD AND NEW RUBY THUMBPRINT GOBLETS, THE ORIGINAL BEING ON THE LEFT. NEW SHOE, AND COPY OF STAFFORDSHIRE VASE, MADE IN PORTUGAL.

Plate 87

ALL REPRODUCTIONS OF COLORED INVERTED THUMBPRINT,
EXCEPT THE PITCHER ON THE LEFT.

Plate 88

MODERN GOBLETS WHICH ARE NOT COPIES OF DESIGNS IN EARLY GLASS.

Plate 89
MODERN PLATE NOT TO BE CONFUSED WITH ANY OLD ONE.

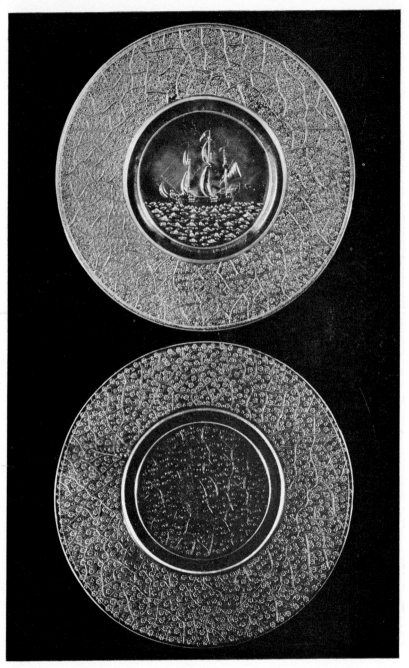

Plate 90
MODERN PLATES, NOT RELATED TO ANY OLD ONES.

Plate 91

Upper: ORIGINAL LACY SANDWICH BEEHIVE PLATE WHICH HAS BEEN
REPRODUCED IN MANY SIZES AND COLORS.

Lower: NEW "LACY SANDWICH" PLATE OF BACCARAT ORIGIN. THIS
DESIGN IS COPIED IN MANY FORMS.

Plate 92
REPRODUCTIONS OF OLD STYLE "SILVERED" OR MERCURY GLASS.

Plate 93

CURTAIN TIEBACKS, JAM JARS, PICKLE JARS, AND VARIOUS OBJECTS
AS INTRODUCED OVER TWENTY-FIVE YEARS AGO.

than because I am sure to have inquiries about it in years to come. Other matching pieces of tableware may be seen in the same design.

There is little demand for the "silvered" or mercury glass today, for all of its high decorative value. This was produced originally by making the objects in thin blown glass which was later coated with mercury on the inside and then the stop or opening where the quicksilver was injected was sealed. If left open to the air the mercury would soon discolor.

On Plate 92 are shown representative pieces of the new glass. A barrelful of this ware was sent out to the Cape a few years ago, and there sold as genuine Sandwich glass. It would be difficult to tell most of the new from the old, except for the obvious appearance of newness. I have never seen any reproductions of silvered curtain tiebacks, though new ones have been made in pressed tin and in the old early Sandwich opal and colored glass for more than twenty-five years. Some of these are illustrated on Plate 93. The stems of the early pieces were always of pewter and since new pewter has more of the appearance of silver plate, it is not difficult to tell them apart.

English Hobnail, originally known as Diamond pattern, is an attractive line of glassware, first made about fifty years ago. It is seen today in department stores and gift shops, for it has always been a popular pattern and has enjoyed a wide sale. Antique shops rarely carry any of it, though I occasionally see a hat in the toothpick holder size in crystal or milk-white. Plate 162.

PATTERN GLASS REPRODUCTIONS

(*Alphabetically Arranged*)

ALPHABET PLATE. Six and a half-inch. Clear and colors. Star center.

ALPHABET PLATE. Six and a half-inch. Clear and colors. Dog's head in center.

ALPHABET PLATE. Six and a half-inch. Clear and colors. Boy's head in center. 1937.

BALTIMORE PEAR. Goblets, plates, sauce dishes. Poor designing in background of the leaves. Clear glass.

BASKETWEAVE. Goblets, clear and colors. Goblet smaller, foot too thin, basketweave poorly executed.

BEADED GRAPE. Goblets and large square plates. Clear glass and emerald green. Leaves on old, thicker and have fine stippling which gives silvery appearance. First bunch of grapes at top of bough has very short stem on old; stem is nearly quarter of an inch long on new. Many faulty details on new.

BELLFLOWER. Water tumbler. Greenish tint, heavy, large design, extra thick base. No ring. This piece is under suspicion. No positive verification now.

BLACKBERRY. Goblets and creamer, in milk-white. First copies of goblet out about 1940. Blurred detail of design. Poor coloring of white, which is not dense white but has pearllike surface. Mold later improved but still detail does not compare favorably with the old.

BLACKBERRY VARIANT. A Blackberry design advertised frequently under the name "Blackberry," is not the one illustrated in *Early American Pressed Glass*. It has long stems with leaves, and single long stems with a single bunch of berries on it, instead of clusters of leaves and berries.

CHERRY. Goblet. Glass appears new and the design is in sharper relief than on the old. Plate 66, *Early American Pressed Glass*. Made in clear and in milk-white. 1937.

CRYSTAL WEDDING. Goblets and covered compotes. Clear, and clear decorated in red. Many of the copies, when placed alongside originals, show a greenish tint. The old may be faintly yellowish. The contours of the steps leading to the knob on the cover are sharper in the old. The almond-pointed thumbprints in the band about the cover are clearly defined and sharp in the new, whereas in the old they appear to run together. Late copies are made in milk-white, decorated in gilt, and advertised as "Golden Wedding." Several sizes in compotes.

DAISY AND BUTTON.

Baby shoe. Four and a half-inch. All colors, including amber, blue, amethyst, marble glass. 1937.

Butter chips. Two and a half inches, round. Clear, amber, yellow, frosted, milk-white, amethyst, two shades of blue. Also, two and seven-eighths inches. Clear, green, milk-white, two shades of blue, amethyst, amber. Possibly other colors. 1937.

Coal bucket match holder. Clear and colors. 1937.

Flask, or bottle. Flattened sides. All-over Daisy and Button. Amethyst, milk-white. Not a copy of a known old flask.

Goblets. The first style copied was the Daisy and Button with Thumbprint, in the 1930's. It has been made in clear glass and all colors. As this goes to press, goblets in this design are reported in amberina. The coloring is a brilliant yellow combined with a bright strawberry-red, which is so different from the old that no one should be deceived by them. Next came the type having three narrow panels in the bowl (Plate 70), in the 1930's. All colors. Then followed the all-over Daisy and Button goblet in clear and colors. Some of the copies have been produced in colors not made originally, such as deep amethyst and sapphire blue. Another goblet with a flat stem, like that pictured on Plate 65, is not a copy of any known old one. It is modern and came out in the 1930's.

Hats. Three inches high, three inches wide. Frosted, yellow, amber, amethyst, green, two shades of blue and probably other colors. 1930's. Celery size hat. Same style as above in five-inch (largest) size. Blue slag, ruby, amberina, yellow, dark blue, amber, and probably other colors. Six inches across.

Hat, spoon holder size. Three and three-quarters inches high, four and three-quarters inches across. Sapphire blue, yellow, amber, and probably full range of colors.

Toothpick holder size. Three inches high, two and three-quarters inches across. Amber, yellow, deep blue. Probably full range of colors.

Small hat. Two and one-half inches high, three and a quarter inches wide. Ruby-red, honey amber, and perhaps other colors.

Small hat. Two and one-eighth inches high, two and three-eighths inches wide. Amber, green, light green, two shades of blue, amethyst, ruby-red, clear

Medium-size hat. Three by three and a quarter inches. Two and three-quarters inches high. Amber, ruby-red, three shades of blue, amethyst, green, clear, yellow and possibly other shades.

Hat, four and a half inches. Amber. Probably full color range.

Hat, two and three-quarters inches tall. Toothpick. Opaque blue, blue.

The variation in sizes and details is due to the fact that these hats have been made by several companies. Many of these came out in the 1930's.

Hand holding cornucopia vase. Six inches. 1930's. Amethyst, yellow, blue, green, clear, and probably other colors.

Plates. Square. Seven inches. 1930's. All colors.

Open fan plates. All colors. 1937. Later style, ten and a half inches wide, seven inches deep. Yellow, amber, clear with frosted handle, amethyst, two shades of blue, green, clear. Not made in this size originally.

Round plate, ten-inch. All colors.

Small round. All colors.

Sauce dish, square. Blue, amber, probably all colors.

Slippers. All-over Daisy and Button. Five and one-half-inch. Amber, yellow, apple-green, frosted, dark blue, light blue, green, honey-amber, ruby-red, and probably other colors.

Puss-in-boots slipper. All over Daisy and Button. Five and three-quarters-inch. Amber, green, amethyst, two shades of blue, yellow, ruby-red, clear, and probably other colors.

Puss-in-boots, five-inch. Alligator toe. Opaque blue, blue, and probably other colors.

Daisy and button, flat bow. Opaque-blue, blue, and probably other colors.

Daisy and Button, four-inch. Amberina.

Slipper, five-inch. Blue slag, amber, deep blue, yellow, ruby, amberina.

Slipper, two-inch. Amber, yellow, blue, amethyst and probably full color range.

Some of the slippers were made in Czechoslovakia during the 1930's. The buttons protrude more on the imports.

Toilet sets, consisting of two small round bottles and powder jar sometimes displayed on open-fan tray. All colors, including amethyst. 1930's.

Tray, in shape of whisk broom. Six-inch. Blue, amber, frosted, milk-white, clear and probably other colors.

Wines and champagnes. Daisy and Button with Thumbprint. Blue, amber, and probably other colors.

Wines and champagnes in all-over Daisy and Button. Often seen in blue; probably full color range.

Daisy and Button with Narcissus, wines.

Vases. Daisy and Button with clear panels. Illustrated Plate 66. This type not known in original pattern. Goblets and bowls (round or oval) to match. 1937. Appeared first in clear glass. Vases, nine and a half to nine and three-quarters inches high. Yellow, amber, green, aquamarine, deep blue, clear. 1937.

Daisy and Cube, Plate 69, Victorian glass. Miniature lamp in all colors, including amberina. A goblet in marble glass has been produced, probably from the lamp mold, but is unlike in shape any known marble glass goblet. Wines are also made in the same design.

Diamond Cut with Leaf goblets and wines. 1930's. Poor copies. Glass thinner than originals.

Dew and Raindrop. Goblets, wines, cordials, sherbet cups. Early 1930's.

Diamond Quilted. Goblets. Elongated rounded bowl, short stem, unlike any known old one. Amber, and probably other colors. More than one style, all poor copies. Tumblers. Amber, and probably other colors.

FROSTED COIN toothpick holders. Copy much heavier, stars are larger, and the word "Liberty" is scarcely legible, in the new.

FROSTED CIRCLE. Goblets. Frosted circles appear to have been ground down to shape them, before they were frosted. Glass appears new. Good copy.

FROSTED RIBBON. See Ribbon pattern.

HERRINGBONE goblets. Clear, emerald green. See Plate 164, No. 1, *Early American Pressed Glass.* Light in weight, exceedingly poor color. The shade is not the correct deep emerald-green.

HOBNAIL

On Plate 56 are shown pieces in shapes that were never made in the old Hobnail pattern. This is gift shop merchandise, that came out about 1930. On Plates 57 and 58 are additional styles, not made in early glass. 1930.

Barber bottles. Two styles, round bowl, and with straight sides. Differences in size and placing of hobnails, and in neck of the bottles.

Bottles. Nine-inch. Blown hobnail, with twisted handle. 1937.

Bowls. Seven-inch. Cranberry, blown, with ruffled edge. Probably additional sizes and colors.

Finger bowls with ruffled edges, unlike any known old ones.

Cruets. Two styles, one with round bowl, having large hobnail. Second, with straight sides and small hobnails. Both carry hobnail stoppers.

Creamers. See pitchers.

Goblets.

1. Opal. A full line of tableware in this pattern, including plates with scalloped edges, wines, etc. was carried by a Philadelphia department store, in 1932. They are not, strictly speaking, reproductions, since there is no old pattern to correspond. Goblet shown on Plate 59.

2. New goblet has large bowl and short twisted stem decorated with hobnails. So far it has been seen only in opal and in clear glass. This is not a copy of any known old one.

Lamps.

    1. Eight and a half-inch. All glass, covered with hobnails. Amber and possibly other colors.

    2. Night lamp. Opalescent hobnail.

Pitchers. Many styles and sizes, from creamers to large water pitchers. Creamers are often seen in rose-opalescent, with bulbous body and frilled edge. These are much too heavy and the lip too thick. Water pitchers were made in the same style and have the same failings. A different water pitcher has a bulbous body, frilled edge and hobnails to the very edge of the top. Still another style has a square neck, twice as high as it should be. New creamers and water pitchers have been made unlike any known old ones, an example being the creamer on Plate 60.

Puss-in-boots slipper. Never made originally in Hobnail. May be found in opalescent, milk-white or blue. Possibly other colors.

Salt and pepper shakers. Excellent copies, which came out in crystal and in blue, in 1949.

Tumblers. Two styles, one blown with hobs nearly to top of tumbler. Second has seven rows of hobnails. In the old, the hobs are larger around at the base, larger in size and more closely set together. New ones seen most often in blue. These came out during the early 1940's.

Horn of Plenty. Water tumbler. This came out about 1933 in clear glass. Sets were made later in amber. No ring. Diamond points are too sharp. Ground-out pontil of old is simulated by pressed depression in new. Good copy. Lamp bowls in a dark blue and in clear, set usually in milk-white bases, appeared in the 1930's. These are exceedingly poor and should not deceive any careful buyer. Freaks produced from the mold of the new tumbler may be seen on Plate 44.

Icicle. Goblet. Modern; bearing no resemblance to the genuine old goblet, known by that name. 1938.

Inverted Thumbprint.

Bowls, eleven inches in diameter, five inches high, frilled edge, collared base. Clear with opal dots. Probably other sizes and colors. See finger bowls.

Creamer. Four and a half inches. Folded top. Blue, green, amethyst. Probably other colors.

Creamer. Tankard shape. Four-inch. Cranberry with opal dots, clear handle. Probably other colors.

Cranberry-colored creamers, frilled top.

Cruets. Cranberry, with clear stoppers. Rose-red with opal dots. Blue with opal dots. Probably other colors.

Flip glass. Eight-inch. Clear and colors. Not made originally.

Finger bowls. Sapphire-blue, cranberry. Probably other colors. Thumbspots always too large and glass too heavy.

Goblet. Straight-sided bowl, knob stem. Amber and probably other colors. Two other modern styles have been made, unlike any corresponding old ones.

Night lamp. Four inches to top of collar. Clear with opalescent dots. Probably other colors.

Pitchers. Water. Folded top. Nine-and-a-half-inch. Blue, green, amethyst, and assorted colors.

Pitcher, frilled top, ribbed handle. Large dots. Clear, with opal dots. Probably other colors. Tumblers to match. Four-inch.

Pitcher, bulbous. Reeded handle. Cranberry with opal dots. Probably assorted colors.

Rose bowl. Six-inch.

Tumblers. Cranberry-red. Four-inch, frosted, with opal dots. Amber. Probably assorted colors.

Ivy in Snow. New sets were out in 1937 in clear glass, with a few items being done in milk-white, such as table set (butter dish, creamer, spoon holder, sugar bowl) and celery vases. Complete sets have been produced by another company during the 1940's, in milk-white. None of this milk-white achieves the density of white of the old. Copies are good but have what some term a "ricey" appearance. In the clear, the stippling is thinner than in the old pieces.

King's Crown. This is Ruby Thumbprint without the red coloring. Goblets; wines in two styles; one flaring at top, and the second like the old ones; tumblers; small tumbler (not made originally); champagnes; sherbets (a footed sauce dish like a small compote, not made originally), and ten-and-a-half-inch covered compote. Late 1930's and 1940's. *See* Ruby Thumbprint.

LACE DEWDROP. Goblet. Clear and milk-white. Claimed to be made from original mold. This is a late pattern, so mold could have been retained. Other pieces also came out in the late 1930's, including sugar bowl, creamer, spoon holder, and butter dish. Another company is now making large sets in this pattern, in milk-white. The earlier milk-white goblets were not really white. Latest modern ones are a better white. Plate 96.

"LACY SANDWICH" goblet. Modern goblet, unlike the "Lacy Sandwich" sold in department stores and described in the chapter on pattern glass. Evidently this name was used on lists, for a time, by certain agents to attract mail buyers who are misled by the designation. This pattern matches a plate once sold in ten-cent stores. Illustrated on Plate 88.

LEAF sauce dish. Shaped like a small leaf and not footed. Clear and colors. 1937.

LION goblets, sugar bowl, creamer, spoon holder, butter dish, sauce dish (four-inch), oval covered compote, eggcups, celery vase, round bread plates. Possibly other pieces. New goblets may be identified by the lion's mouth. On the old, it is a straight even line on all three faces. On the new, one mouth is twisted down at one corner. Detail is poor on most of the pieces, and frosting too white.

LORD'S SUPPER plates. Oblong bread tray in a late design, made first in Pittsburgh area. Copies came out in the 1930's, first in clear glass and later, frosted.

MARBLE GLASS. The copies in this ware should not deceive careful buyers. During the 1940's there appeared in this coloring, seven-inch covered hen dishes (Plate 97), Atterbury ducks, slippers, baby's shoe, and a covered sugar and creamer with fruit on the side panels. The coloring has all been much too light and too blurred.

MAPLE LEAF goblets. Extremely poor copies of a rare goblet. Stem much too thick, clear and colors.

MOON AND STAR. Goblets came out first in the late 1930's. These were followed in the early 1940's by eggcups, footed sauce dishes, and a miniature night lamp made from eggcup mold. No such lamp was made originally. Then covered compotes appeared in color, often blue-opalescent. New colored goblets came next, followed by clear champagnes, salt dips, covered butter, spoon holders, sugar bowls, footed tumblers, water pitcher, plates in sizes seven, eight and ten inches, punch bowl and punch cups, and miniature lamps in color, with matching colored shades. This pattern was made only in clear glass originally. Whale oil lamps have been advertised lately with the fonts in blue or clear glass but these are not true Moon and Star pattern.

NEW ENGLAND PINEAPPLE. Goblets and cordials. No ring to glass. Cordial has no ring, foot is too small and too thin. 1937.

OVERLAY, "Spot Resist." This is a pressed imitation of the more expensive cut overlay glass. It is most often seen with a thin layer of white glass over pink, with round pink "spots."
Barber bottles. Tankard pitchers in cranberry and in blue.
Cruets. Bulbous vases, with frilled tops. Undoubtedly many other novelty items.

OPAL FRUIT GOBLET. Not a reproduction since these were never made in old glass. A design which is very similar, except that the stems of the goblets are reeded, is made in sets of tableware and is called Della Robbia. The latter is made in clear glass, clear and partly frosted, and clear with painted or enameled colors. Plate 59.

OPAL CURTAIN TIEBACKS. Early Sandwich styles have been successfully copied, though the old ones always had pewter stems and the new stems are not at all convincing. The knobs themselves look new. Different colors. Reproductions first came out about 1910. Plate 93.

PANELED GRAPE. Goblet reproductions were on the market during the 1930's. The wines followed at about the same time.

Since then a whole set has been made. Known reproductions include the water pitcher, parfaits, butter dish, celery vase, creamer, sherbet cups, lemonade glass, sauce dish, sugar bowls, spoon holder, plates, tumblers, wines and cordials. In the old the leaf is in heavier relief and is finely, heavily stippled. In the new, there is very little stippling on the leaves. This pattern was made in clear glass originally. Copies of the goblets are out in several colors, including amethyst, emerald-green, milk-white, opalescent, ruby, etc.

PANELED THISTLE. Goblets appeared first, followed by plates, champagnes, and wines. The goblet was out early in 1940. The style copied is the one with flaring bowl. Square seven-inch plates were made, followed by the ten-inch round ones. Other unreported sizes may also be on the market. It is such a late pattern it is possible that the copies are made from old molds. The only way to detect the modern is in the quality and weight of the glass, together with its new appearance.

PLEAT AND PANEL. Goblets and seven-inch plates. Foot of the old goblet is thicker and cupped higher. In the paneled window on the bowl, the stippling is much lighter and not so evenly distributed as on the copies. In the new one this panel stands out like a windowpane, with a higher edge to the panel. Same faulty stippling applies to the plates.

RED BLOCK. Goblets and wines. Newness is apparent in the color of the red in the red blocks.

RIBBON. Goblets. 1945. This is the early one having an indented panel alternating with the heavy frosted one. The frosting is much too rough to the touch, and many of the panels show marks as if filed or treated with some rough tool in achieving the finish.

ROMAN ROSETTE. Goblets. 1945. Foot too thin. Stippling too even and too light, without the finely pebbled appearance of the old. Glass is light and poor in color.

ROSE IN SNOW. Goblets and plates. 1930's. Clear and colors. Detail of little leaves missing in first copy of goblet. This was supplied later but inserted wrongly, with smaller of two missing leaves clinging to the larger one below. Plates are too thin, stippling too light.*

RUBY THUMBPRINT. Goblets, tumblers, wines, "cocktails" (wines with flaring bowl) lemonades (not made originally) small tumbler (not made originally) and sherbets (not made originally). The sherbets are footed sauce dishes, on a fairly high stem, like a little compote. The new may be identified in most cases by the copper tinting in the applied red coloring. The shade of red is not correct in the copies.

SHELL AND TASSEL. Goblet. 1930's. Excellent copy. New ones may be easily identified by holding goblet to the light and looking through enclosed ornament which connects the large shell design. The clear center of this ornament is perfectly clear in the old but the glass has a "wavy" appearance in the new.

"SILVERED" OR MERCURY GLASS. 1930's. Barrels full of this ware were once shipped to Cape Cod and sold there as genuine old Sandwich glass. Some of it is still made today, like the pieces illustrated. The old would always show evidences of age. Plate 92.

SPANISH LACE. 1940's. Finger bowls, water pitchers, tumblers, creamers, cruets, sugar shakers, lamp shades. Several colors, including blue, rose, and cranberry.

SPRAY AND CANE. This is a late plate, so late that it is probably being made from an old mold. The modern ones can be identified by the new appearance of the glass. Plate 68. Other matching forms are also made, in clear and colors.

STAR WITH DEWDROP. 1934. Seven and a quarter-inch plates and salts. It is possible to catch the fingernail on the edge of the rim on the base of the old. These were made only in clear glass originally. Colored plates are now on the market. The footed salts came out about 1934. See text for differences between old and new. These were also made only in clear glass originally but the market has been flooded with them in many shades of

---

* New "In fond Remembrance" mugs appeared in 1950. Good copies but the stippling is too white and too thin.

color, including amethyst. Later, handles were attached to the salts, thus forming little baskets. These are strictly modern.

STRAWBERRY AND CURRANT. 1940. Goblets in clear, amber, blue, yellow, and possibly other colors. Very poor detail in the leaves and berries. All the seeds show prominently in the old berries but are few and far between in the new. This goblet was made only in clear glass originally. Plate 84.

THOUSAND EYE. 1940. Goblets, eight-inch square plates, cruets, twine holders, and tumblers. Clear and colors. The goblets are the most difficult fakes to detect and since the means of doing so is involved, it is suggested that the reader study the text for the differences. The "eyes" are heavier and the corners more carefully executed in the old plates. Tumblers have been advertised but I have not seen them, so purchasers should have a guarantee with any they buy. They are listed in clear, amber and amberina, the last being a color they were never made in originally. Parfaits are also listed but they are modern. The cruets are unlike the old ones in shape, and have round stoppers. The twine holders are also different in shape than the originals.

THREE PANEL. 1949. There have been persistent rumors that these goblets are out but I have not seen them. Usually the copies are too light, particularly the foot.

THREE FACE. Goblets, footed sauce dishes, covered butter dish (six-inch, on pedestal), champagnes in three styles (1. saucer, 2. deep bowl, 3. hollow stem) lamps, and possibly other pieces. 1939–1940. The frosting is too white and often, though not always, harsh to the touch. Details are poor, particularly the noses, which are not sharp enough. All old Three Face is a gray-white and the faces appear alive when held to a strong light. The new lamp has a scalloped foot and round, clear bowl.

THUMBPRINT. Goblet. 1930's. A modern goblet, unlike any of the known early ones in that pattern. Elongated thumbprint with double knob stem; soft lime glass with no ring to it. Wines and tumblers to match, in clear and colors.

TULIP. Wines. 1940. The old have a thick foot and large knob stem. The copies are thinner, the knob stem small and the foot too thin and smaller.

TURKEY JAM JARS. On the market since the early 1920's. Originally made in one large size in crystal, or in clear glass painted over in natural colors, the new ones appear in three sizes, and in colors, including green, salmon-pink, and amber. A small size measures two and three-quarters inches high. The original jar is the largest of the three sizes and carries much finer detail.

WAFFLE. Goblet. 1938. A modern goblet bearing no resemblance to the old one known by that name. Listing it by mail under a false name attracted buyers. Plate 88.

WESTWARD-HO. 1936–40. Goblets, footed sauce dishes, oval covered compotes, round covered compotes on high foot, water pitchers, wines, and possibly other pieces. The new goblet may easily be identified by the mouth of the deer. It is blurred, as if biting into foliage, on the copy, and a perfectly straight sealed line on the old. Detail is poor on all pieces, and the frosting much too white. The old is a gray-white, with fine detail work. Every hair is in place on the deer, much like a fine engraving, in all old pieces.

WILDFLOWER. 1936. Goblets, large square plates, and tumblers. Goblets appeared first, in clear and in colors. The design was much too thin. A new mold was apparently made and then the design was produced too thick and compact. The stem goes directly through the cluster of some of the four berries in the new. The shades of color are too harsh. The old yellow and blue were soft, mellow, pastel shades. The berries and flowers are larger and more compact in the new plates. Curiously, most of the old plates weigh one and three-quarters pounds and the new ones weigh two pounds. A number of the new plates I have seen, have scratches on some of the panels, possibly to suggest wear. Additional pieces may be on the market, which I have not seen.

Chapter VII

MILK-WHITE GLASS

There are more reproductions of milk-white glass today than in any other line, or pattern, in the pressed glass field. Two or three companies are making it a specialty. Gift shops and some department stores have quantities of it on sale. All any collector or dealer need do is visit some of the shops carrying this ware and study it. An experienced eye will soon detect differences so obvious that the reproductions will cease to be a worry. Practically all of it is too heavy in weight, when contrasted with their older mates. Again, the whiteness is not the white of the earlier ware. The objective in making what the old-time glassworkers always referred to as "Opal" (with the accent on the second syllable), was to achieve a dense white glass. It was referred to in the beginning as "hot caste porcelain." When some ingredients in the batch burned out and left opaline streaks, the workmen would say it had "gone flinty." Thus in creating what was really a dense white, closely resembling china, the old-timers accomplished a result which I have not so far noted in the modern copies. The white in the reproductions varies from a pearllike white, to that which some refer to as "ricey," because it resembles the coloring in uncooked rice. Sometimes, though not always, the new has more gloss to the surface. Collectors who are seeking old milk-white glass should carry a genuine sauce dish, or any other small piece, about with them for contrast. It is the density of whiteness that counts, in the originals.

Sometimes the early ware did have opaline streaks, or an opal quality noticeable in the edges of dishes, but it is the general character of the whiteness that must be watched.

There is no harm whatsoever in all these reproductions, when they are sold as such. Some pocketbooks cannot stand the strain

177

of the high-priced originals and so many homemakers can indulge in the highly decorative modern pieces at a comparatively low figure. The effect is much the same! Unfortunately, too much of the modern finds its way into antique shops.

Just as long as there are dealers who are unscrupulous; just as long as there are dealers who are too indifferent or too lazy to inform themselves as to the obvious differences between new and old examples; and just as long as there are gullible and ill-informed collectors, there will be plenty of counterfeits.

One may argue that firms deliberately putting out glass reproductions to be sold as antiques are in the minority; that for every peddler of such wares there are a hundred honest "pickers"; and that dealers buying such merchandise are the exception rather than the rule. Well, burglars are a minority group, but I doubt if knowledge of the fact is much comfort to the man who has just been relieved of his silver collection or his wife's jewelry. Of course, if he has provided himself with burglar insurance, he is not without consolation; and as for the burglar, the arm of the law usually gathers him in sooner or later.

The best insurance the glass dealer or collector can carry is a working knowledge of the main differences between old and new glass, along with detailed information about the various counterfeits as they appear. Stopping the practice of antique glass counterfeiting is not easy, however, since it thrives on the less-pleasing human traits—greed and gullibility. Barnum made a fortune out of the latter, but he gave his victims their money's worth in entertainment. I doubt if anyone ever got much pleasure out of paying an antique price for a modern piece of glass.

In weighing an old and a new milk-white plate, I found the new weighed two ounces more than the old. In pattern glass there is often a wider variance. A new Wildflower plate weighed a quarter of a pound more than an old one. A new cranberry Inverted Thumbprint tumbler weighed half a pound and an original like it weighed a quarter of a pound. There is a much greater difference in the weight of old and new cranberry pitchers. So weighing glass is one more way of detecting copies.

Plate 94
NEW MILK-WHITE GLASS.

Plate 95

MODERN MILK-WHITE RABBIT AND KITTEN PLATES.

NEW LACE DEWDROP GOBLET.

MODERN SATIN GLASS VASE.

Plate 96

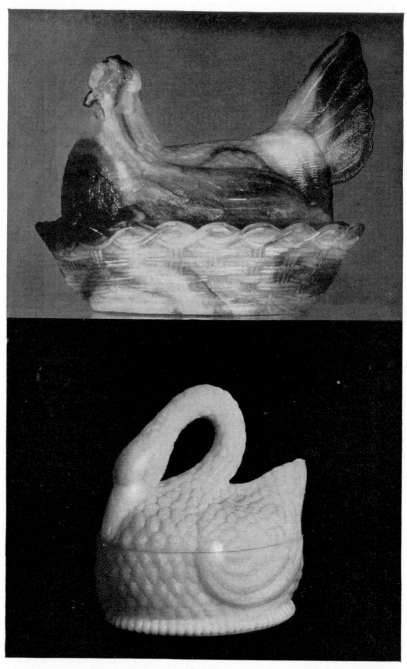

Plate 97
Upper: REPRODUCTION HEN DISH IN PURPLE MARBLE GLASS.
Lower: VALLERYSTHAL FIVE-AND-ONE-QUARTER-INCH SWAN
COVERED DISH.

It would be impractical to attempt to enumerate the differences between each and every one of the vast quantity of old and new milk-white items, since I have pointed out the distinguishing characteristics of the modern pieces.

I shall attempt to give the reader as complete a listing of the reproductions as possible, for easy reference. There is a chance that I have missed some, particularly since fakes are sometimes made up for a few certain dealers who own control of the mold, and thus they can disperse them slowly. Study your glass and be careful.

ANIMAL DISHES

ATTERBURY DUCK. Eleven-inch. A large variety of colors, including amethyst, marble glass, jade green, milk-white and white with colored heads. New ones are always undated.

CAMEL. This was made originally by Vallerysthal, in Alsace. The factory is said to have been destroyed during the last war, so some of their dishes are now being made here. Marked pieces would be old.

CAT. On rectangular lace-edged base. Milk-white, opaque-blue.

DOG. Ribbed base. Milk-white.

FROG. This is not like McKee dish. It is a sitting frog, and old ones are marked VALLERYSTHAL.

HAND WITH DOVE. Rectangular base with lace edge.

HENS. Basket weave base, five- and seven-inch sizes. Made in Marble glass, amberina, in white with colored heads, in opaque-blue, amber, amethyst and milk-white. Some of these were sold during the early 1930's. Plates 94, 97.

HENS. Varied sizes and coloring, chiefly in two-, three-, and four- and one-half-inch sizes. Colors, milk-white, amber, opaque-blue, black, and probably others. Have seen a frosted green.

ROOSTERS. On basket weave base, five- and seven-inch. Milk-white, frosted, opaque-blue. Sometimes sold with addition of glass eyes. Also, on a ribbed base, five-inch.

CHICKEN ON BASKET with handles. Milk-white. Plate 94.

STANDING ROOSTER. Originally a Vallerysthal covered dish. Milk-white, opaque-blue.

ROBIN. Vallerysthal, on elaborate base, a pedestal type. Shown in *Victorian Glass,* Plate 116.

DUCK. Milk-white, frosted, five-inch.

As this goes to press, copies of the five-inch duck on a split rib base, have come on the market.

DUCK. Squatty type, six-inch, frosted and probably colors.

RABBIT, MULE-EARED. Basket weave base. Five-inch. Milk-white, milk-white with jade green head.

RECLINING RABBIT. Basket weave base. Seven-inch. Milk-white, opaque-blue.

RABBIT. Picket base, five-inch.

RABBIT. Split rib base.

SWAN. Uplifted wings. Rectangular base with lace edge. Nine-and-one-half-inch.

SWAN. Open neck, five-and-one-half-inch. Clear, frosted, milk-white. Vallerysthal. Plate 97.

SWAN. Open neck, five-inch. Basket weave base.

LARGE FISH. Vallerysthal. Frosted green, among other colors.

LARGE TURTLE. Vallerysthal, eight-inch. Milk-white, amber.

TURKEY. McKee type, with split rib base. Milk-white and colors. Five-inch.

PLATES

The set of plates decorated with kittens, owls, rabbits, etc., are said to have been souvenirs of the Pan-American Exposition held in Buffalo, N. Y. in 1901. These listed are being made today, and some were also available during the 1930's. Sets were sometimes sold, held together with colored ribbons. Plate 95.

THREE BEARS
EASTER CHICKS
THREE KITTENS
THREE OWLS
RABBIT AND HORSESHOE

CUPID AND PSYCHE
GEORGE WASHINGTON
INDIAN HEAD
NIAGARA FALLS
CONTRARY MULE
ANCHOR AND YACHT
ANGEL
OLD CASTLE

LACE-EDGED PLATES

Old glassworkers used to refer to these as "O.W." plates (open-work).

HEART. Two sizes. One new batch was made in red, perhaps on special order.

SQUARE "S" edge. Eight and one-half, nine and one-half inches.

FLEUR-DE-LIS, EAGLE AND FLAG. Seven-inch.

WICKET. Nine-inch.

SQUARE, peg border, eight-inch.

FOR-GET-ME-NOT. Seven-, eight-inch.

FLEUR-DE-LIS. Seven-inch.

LATTICE edge ten-and-one-half-inch plates with both open and closed edge. These have just been reported, so I have not seen them. They are said to be rather poor copies, being heavy and with a "ricey" appearance.

MILK-WHITE PATTERN GLASS

BLACKBERRY goblets and creamer. These are copies of the true Blackberry pattern. Plate 71.

BLACKBERRY VARIANT. Not a pattern known to collectors and dealers. This is a design you will see in department stores. It is plain, having one long stem with a single cluster of leaves, and three shorter stems, each carrying one berry.

LACE DEWDROP. Some dealers are now referring to this as "Beaded Dewdrop." It has been made off and on since about

1900. Fairly large sets are now being produced in milk-white. Plate 96.

IVY IN SNOW. Made almost exclusively in crystal originally, it is now being turned out in sets, in milk-white. Modern pieces have been in production, off and on, since the 1930's.

MOON AND STAR VARIANT. Bowls, eight-inch. Footed compote, eight inches high.

ENGLISH HOBNAIL. This design was originated by Mr. Charles West, who founded the Westmoreland Glass Co. about 1893. It was made by him, mostly in crystal, while he was associated with the company. A number of pieces are now being made in milk-white, including compotes, rose bowls, covered sugar bowls, baskets, goblets, and other modern forms. Plate 162.

BLOCK AND FAN VARIANT. Covered compotes, water pitcher, lemonade glasses (tall tumblers) sugar bowls, vases, etc. Plate 94.

SWAN (with Fern). A few attractive pieces are being turned out in this pattern, such as butter dishes, matchholders, etc.

SWAN (with cattails). Items in this design have been in circulation since the 1930's. There are covered sugars, covered creamers (Swan finial) a tall vase, matchholders and possibly other items.

GRAPE. A modern milk-white grape goblet, having a heavy design of grapes, with fine lines about the stem, appeared in the 1920's, and department stores carried them. Some had grapes on the inside of the bowl. A similar Grape pattern has been carried on in water pitchers and lemonade tumblers, besides the goblet.

MAPLE LEAF. Copies of a very late pattern, in a two-handled sugar and a creamer, with an all-over leaf design. This is not the Maple Leaf illustrated in *Early American Pressed Glass*.

CHERRIES. A covered sugar and creamer in a very late pattern, having flat panels on the sides showing a cluster of cherries. These have also appeared in a poor copy of Marble glass.

WILD ROSE. Covered sugars and creamers. Gift shop items.

PEACOCK. Covered sugars and creamers. Gift shop items.

FRUIT. Known in stores as Della Robbia. A modern set of glass made in crystal, in milk-white, and in crystal painted over in colors. Plate 59.

In addition, there are duck open salts, a ribbed covered compote with openwork edge on foot; ribbed sugar bowls; two sizes in the large deep shell supported by a dolphin with hexagonal base, and the same type dolphin base supporting a round bowl; several styles of vases (lily of the valley, wild rose, etc.) ; fifteen- and nine-and-one-half-inch vases, in a large flower pattern, or a grape pattern, which are copies of old-time pickle jars (Plate 93) ; lace-edged compotes, cake plates and candlesticks (openwork edge around foot) ; double-hand dishes in milk-white, marble glass, and copper luster; Fan and Circle bowl, with or without a collared foot; and a Crystal Wedding covered compote in milk-white, sometimes decorated in gilt with colored grapes and referred to as "Golden Wedding." A rectangular lace-edged dish is made, eight by four inches, and some dealers advertise an oval seven-inch lace-edged one that will fit some of the animal covers. There are also shell-shaped sauce dishes on three feet, together with a large matching flat fruit bowl. Dolphin candlesticks and a copy of the small Sawtooth candlestick shown in *Early American Pressed Glass* (Plate 40) have been out for years. During the past five years, a number of novelties have appeared in milk-white, which date from the early 1900's, in the way of pin boxes, dresser boxes, round pomades, dresser trays in various sizes and patterns, which were often decorated, during the hand-painted china era, with roses, violets, pansies, etc. A swan salt (Plate 146) appeared during the 1930's, in a pearly white, which showed every indication of newness. These have been seen in a variety of colors, including ruby-red and sapphire-blue. Old ones were made in milk-white during the 1880's.

This is as thorough a listing of milk-white items as it is possible to make at this time. Collectors and dealers must not be careless in their buying, for new pieces are continually coming out.

Chapter VIII

PAPERWEIGHTS

It would be wise for beginners to devote time and study to old paperweights in order to know what the essential points of really fine weights are before going into collecting them on an extensive scale. There are many reproductions on the market, and they have been made not only in this country but also in China, Czechoslovakia, England and other countries.

A brief résumé of the history of old paperweights may be of benefit to new collectors—and perhaps even to some veterans.

To date, I have been unable to find reliable records of when and where the first paperweights were made. My guess would be that they became necessary only after paper came into general use for correspondence, superseding parchment. The first makers may well have worked in Italy. The word "Millefiori" has been associated with paperweights as far back as there are any records of them at all, and Millefiori is Italian for "thousand flowers." The technique of using sections of canes for decorative purposes goes back to ancient Egypt. The Venetian glassmakers knew the art and they made glass for the mosaic workers who not only did floors and house interiors but fine jewelry. The finest type of Millefiori weights were made at St. Louis in Alsace-Lorraine while those provinces were still French, between 1840 and 1851. Certainly some beautiful designs are found bearing the tiny letters *S L* for St. Louis. At Clichy, also in France, other very fine weights were turned out, marked with a tiny *C*. From Clichy the art of making choice paperweights moved on to Baccarat, France. Weights from this town are sometimes marked "B-1847" or "B-1848."

Foreign workmen came to this country to introduce the art and to teach it to American glassworkers. The New England Glass Company at Cambridge, Mass., the Boston & Sandwich Glass Company at Cape Cod, and others, made many paperweights which are eagerly sought today. The earliest date found on any positively known to have been made in this country is 1852. Occasionally a weight is discovered marked "1852" in one place and, in another "1825," the last two numbers having been transposed. I believe 1852 to be the correct date. These are attributed to Sandwich.

There is nothing more difficult for a writer on antiques to describe adequately than paperweights. Try and see if you can do justice with words to the glass, the design, the color and scintillating beauty of the whole!

For the benefit of new collectors, I am illustrating six antique paperweights, all of them desirable and some of the finest workmanship. On Plate 98 the one at each end is a signed and dated "Baccarat, B-1848." In genuine weights the date is so small a magnifying glass is often necessary to find it. The one on the right has a small butterfly in the center and other tiny animals show in the pieces of cane. The Poinsettia in the center paperweight illustrates a good flower type. On Plate 99 another flower is shown with the highly desirable interlaced background. The one at the right is known as a "Crown weight." Study the quality and workmanship as exhibited in these good paperweights and then look at the new ones and wonder how anyone can be fooled!

On Plate 100 are shown some genuinely old pieces of cane, flowers and leaves, such as were used in the making of the better paperweights. The large piece in the foreground is not a stick of Christmas candy but a large fragment of cane showing how such pieces looked before they were stretched out into the tiny rods used in making up the Millefiori weights. You will note in the picture other pieces in the same pattern, graduated in size. The rod or cane was made up with fancy designs in vivid colors running through it, all of which was fused together while it was still plastic. In that state, workmen holding each end on a punty rod, could stretch it out for as much as forty or fifty feet. The "stretch-out" system did not affect the design configuration, which merely grew smaller and smaller in diameter as it was drawn out. The rods, when ready, were then cut up into tiny slices, each showing the pattern as illustrated on Plate 100. The little pieces were fitted together in all sorts of intricate designs. To accomplish this required a very skillful operator. In making a complete paperweight, a gathering of glass was placed into a ring mold and while the molten metal was still hot the tiny cane "setup" was inserted. These setups could be in the intricate and lovely patterns that we see in the finer weights, or perhaps in a rather haphazard manner like those in the so-called "scattered cane," which are fairly common. A gathering of glass or sometimes several gatherings were then rounded over the top of the entire weight. It then had to be annealed and later polished off to a final finish. The thick glass which covered the top magnified the design in the center, adding to its beauty.

In Millville, N. J., there were three brothers by the name of Barber, all of whom were brought up in the glass trade. They were nearly of an age, and all three were trained at the same time in the art of glassmaking. One of them was particularly adept at making paperweights, while the other two were not so skillful in that branch, but cheerfully conceded the superiority of their brother Ralph as an artist and technician. So Ralph Barber made most of the famous Millville Rose paperweights. He did not discontinue making them until shortly before his death. All of the tools he used are now in the possession of Frank S. Schwartz, of Philadelphia, Pa., who purchased them from Mr. Barber's widow. Mr. Barber passed away about sixteen years ago. His brothers, George and Harry, survive.

The Millville Rose was never a commercial product, but was made after hours. Mr. Barber found it impossible to use the ordinary run of color for his rose weights, so he imported both the rose and the red-colored cullet from abroad. He made the roses in yellow, white, rose-pink and red, with and without bases and with or without the green leaves. One, owned by Mr. Frank S. Schwartz, shows in addition a bud. The mortality rate among these rose weights was high. Nearly half of them would crack in cooling. This was due to the fact that the rose was of a different metal. The difference in the coefficients of expansion and contraction developed strains which caused the cracks. It is not uncommon to find one of these damaged weights in antique shops or in private collections, for the Millville Roses have been in such great demand that they have become not only very scarce but when found at all, command a high price.

On Plate 101 is the most interesting "horrible example" I have ever seen anywhere, of a copy of a paperweight. On the left is a beautiful and genuinely old example of the Millville Rose. On the right is one of the first attempts to copy it, which certainly looks like the last rose of Millville!

After the first edition of this book had been on the market for a few months, I learned that bigger and better new rose paperweights were appearing on Pine Street in Philadelphia. The price was $75.00 for three, but the buyer had to take them all. One of this type appears at the extreme right in the illustration on Plate 102. It will be noted that the foot is too small for the ball, though some of the new ones did have a more spreading foot. The rose itself is in a deep and ugly red, shading almost to black. The leaves are a dark green, almost black, and look more like spikes than leaves. The rose is too large, the petals are much too thick, and the whole thing is jammed down into the foot.

One will note also that in all the best of the old rose paperweights, the rose is floated well above the base. The choice old one illustrated at the left end on Plate 102, from the collection of W. Colston Leigh, shows exactly what I mean. Here the rose is a delicate pink, with fragile petals and three well-formed light-green leaves. It is an excellent example of a superlative Millville Rose paperweight.

Later an improved model of the second reproduction rose paperweight appeared on the market. An example of it is shown in the center of Plate 102. It is an improvement over those which showed up first in Philadelphia, and the price also dropped to $15.00 for one. The rose is still red and the petals too thick, but it has four fairly well-shaped green leaves and it is floated a bit above the foot. The shape and proportions are better, but the color of the glass is wrong. In fact, with any of this series of new rose paperweights it is distinctly green instead of a clear, mellow white. This greenish tint appears to be a curious reflection from the coloring of the metal itself. All in all, while the copyists had not yet attained their goal, still both dealers and collectors had been deceived into paying prices ranging from $95.00 to $110.00 each for these counterfeits.

After World War II some better Millville Roses appeared. Also, quite a series were made in a small size, unknown originally, in a wide variety of colors, including red, rose-pink, blue, white, yellow, and very likely other shades. These had beautifully formed flowers placed over four striped green leaves, the latter showing a credible amount of dew. The four leaves are placed directly against the base, instead of being floated well above it, in true Barber style. Perfume bottles were also put out, with one or two roses in the stoppers.

The Barbers also produced a "mushroom" paperweight, as illustrated on Plate 103. On the left is a reproduction of the old one shown on the right. The great difference between them is not so noticeable in the picture as in the actual weights, but still one can note the lack of skillful workmanship. The one on the right is a finely fluted mushroom, decorated with a careful sprinkling of color. The new one is shallow, like an umbrella, and coarse and crude in every particular. The old Millville Mushrooms were made with or without bases, similar in shape to Millville Roses.

On the same illustration is shown a new paperweight perfume bottle. Larger ones were on the market a few years ago. They had a cane background and were dated 1848 in type one could not miss seeing from a distance. I once saw a collector purchase one of the latter at an antique show for $75.00, which he said he intended to present to a museum! New styles of these bottles have been on the market for years, though old ones are still to be found.

In my own collection is another paperweight made by Ralph Barber, which contains colorful bars of cane placed horizontally. In the center is the name KIZZIE PEPPER, MILVILLE, N. J. This was evidently intended as a gift to "Kizzie."

Plate 98

THREE RARE OLD PAPERWEIGHTS. THOSE AT ENDS ARE DATED BACCARAT.

Plate 99

THREE CHOICE OLD PAPERWEIGHTS.

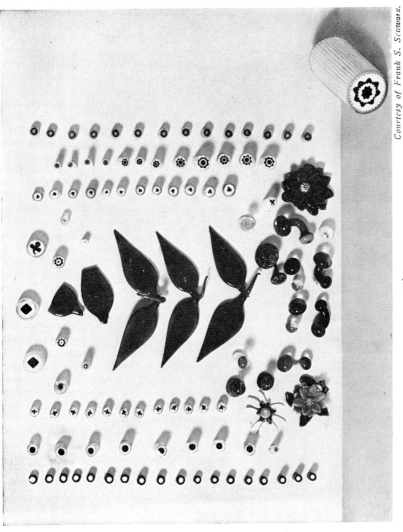

Plate 100

PIECES USED IN GENUINE OLD PAPERWEIGHTS.

Plate 101

ON THE LEFT. GENUINE MILLVILLE ROSE. ON THE RIGHT. FIRST ATTEMPT TO COPY IT.

Plate 102

OLD MILLVILLE ROSE AT LEFT. WITH TWO COPIES.

Plate 103

FAKE MUSHROOM PAPERWEIGHT ON THE LEFT. OLD ONE ON RIGHT.
MODERN PAPERWEIGHT PERFUME BOTTLE IN CENTER.

Along about 1938 the Consolidated Lamp and Glass Company at Coraopolis, Pennsylvania, had in their employ a Mr. Emil Constantine, who was taught the art of making paperweights as a boy, in Alsace-Lorraine. He migrated to this country as a young man and worked at the Pennsylvania factory for nearly fifty years. At seventy-seven years of age, he was still making paperweights. A doorstop and a paperweight which he made in 1939, now in the author's possession, are illustrated on Plate 104. Good paperweight-makers, like good cooks, seem to be born and not made. One man may be very good at blowing glass and yet lack completely the skill required to make fine paperweights. With most of them it is really a sort of pastime occupation, for it entails much "puttery" and tedious work. In the type of weight Mr. Constantine made, the hot glass was gradually gathered, layer by layer. In between the gatherings the glass was worked and paddled to keep it in the proper shape. Also between the gatherings, the designs in colored glass were inserted. They, in turn, were well worked into the hot metal before the next gathering of crystal glass. After completion, twenty-four hours' annealing is required in order to prevent fracture. After the reheating or annealing process, the items were passed to the cutting room where the entire ball was polished before shipping.

Mr. Constantine taught an apprentice the art of making these paperweights, but the president of the company told me it would not be surprising if it required another two years before the pupil could acquire his master's skill.

On the same Plate 104, at the extreme left, is an imported weight believed to have come from Italy. It is really more attractive than it would appear from the picture. The petaled ornament in the center is a deep rose-pink. Were it not for the unfortunate background of the base it rests in, it might easily be taken for a true antique.

There was a time when collectors felt that a pontil mark was the only real evidence of age in a piece of glass. By pontil, I mean the rough scar left on many old pieces of glass where it was broken away from the punty rod when it was cooled and the sharp edges were not smoothed away or ground off. Pontil marks are seen on many fakes to impress novices. As a matter of fact, the bases of most of the finer paperweights are clearly polished or may have a star cut in them. It is best to avoid most paperweights which have a frosted base. Many new ones are frosted. The oldest with this type of base would not be over fifty or sixty years old.

Avoid weights with some pieces of the colored candy protruding above the level of the others. The surface of the colored cane runs smoothly across the center on the old ones. To make this test, hold the paperweight up sideways and look through it. Many of the late Chinese imports are of this variety.

Be particularly careful in purchasing snowstorm paperweights. These have been reproduced at intervals for many years. I have never seen but one such genuine old weight. About twenty years ago, a certain antique dealer bought a number of the fakes. Over each base he pasted a piece of very old calico on the theory that the cloth would date the glass. He took these weights into the country and traded them to housewives for any really old article that they were willing to part with. It is easy to imagine what any attic-rummaging collector would believe if he came across one of these calico-dated snowstorms! The family would not be likely to remember where it came from or when. Many a fake has been innocently passed along by the second generation. On rare pieces today it pays to consult someone known to be both experienced and reliable.

The Chinese weights all look quite different from any of those emigrating from other countries. They are in a class by themselves and it is not a high class! When the Japanese army moved in no Chinese paperweights moved out. Now the story has repeated itself.

To me the quality of the glass in the Chinese weights looks softer. Fine weights have a hard brilliance to which is added the excellence of the workmanship in the colored part. Possibly it is the somewhat blurred effect in the new ones combined with a certain haziness of detail due to the poor quality of the glass which gives the whole weight a different look. It is extremely difficult for the written word to make plain what could be shown so easily on the object itself. A Chinese weight before me now has been carefully ground on the base to give an appearance of age. Natural wear would not be rough. The weights on Plate 105 are Chinese. The one with the four-petaled flower has an unattractive looseness of detail. The largest one is the most typical of their work and the smaller cane type shows the protruding pieces which I have mentioned before.

On Plate 106 is an English reproduction, dated in the center, 1848. In the genuine weight the date is in such tiny letters that it is difficult to find without a magnifying glass. This reproduction would be better if the oversized date had been smaller. It would not deceive an expert who examined it with care. For fineness of detail, it is the best of the reproductions. Another, very similar, is dated 1815, at which period no dated paperweights are known to have been made. In any event, none has survived.

On the same plate at the left is an attractively colored weight of a type which was once largely circulated through Ohio. The background is a coarse yellow- and rose-colored cane. A small flower with stem and leaves floats above it. The base has been very delicately frosted and then scratched up to give it an appearance of years of wear. The third paperweight in this group is Chinese in the same blurred cane effect.

On Plate 107 is a crude attempt at copying a butterfly. It is practically impossible to photograph clearly those details which would show the striking differences between this new one and an old one. It behooves collectors and dealers to study both old and new specimens and even then collectors would be well advised to ask for a money-back guarantee when buying. The dealer could protect himself by agreeing to leave all disputes as to authenticity to the verdict of a recognized authority. Too many collectors have been led into believing a genuine article to be spurious by other disgruntled dealers or by those oversuspicious and ignorant friends who enjoy taking the joy out of a collector's life.

Pictured on Plates 107 and 108 are two paperweights which are colorful and attractive enough to entrap the unwary. In these one

must be guided by the workmanship. The cane is much larger than
is ever seen in many old ones. Also, they are more shallow.

On Plate 108 at the right is an attempt to make a paperweight
with an interlaced background. The result is sad. I am not certain
where this was made but I suspect it was Czechoslovakia. It has
colored cane and is faceted on the top and sides, but it is not at
all convincing. Its powers of deception cannot extend beyond
inexperienced buyers. But friends assure me that they have seen
better ones.

Illustrated on Plate 109 is a paperweight in a fruit pattern, all
of the design being executed in a silver coloring. As far as is
known there are no similar types in really old ones. The same
maker uses various other silvery centers in the shape of lizards,
bees, flowers, birds, etc. An additional such weight, carrying a
rooster, may be seen on Plate 146.

Last and, I might say, least are two paperweights shown on
Plate 110, which were made near Boston, Mass., during the 1930's.
The story told me by one who visited the house where these were
being made at the time, was that an elderly but experienced workman from a New England glass factory produced them over a
gas stove in the kitchen. The visitor claimed these new weights,
which are strictly modern and in no sense reproductions of old
ones, were ornamented with little white pigs or pink birds, which
were broken from the top of ornamental glass pens which came
in from Japan. He purchased some of the pens ornamented with
the birds and pigs, which I still own. Varicolored flowers were
interspersed among the pigs in the weights. Usually the weights
containing the birds showed three, of an unclassified species, gazing
into a nest in which three tiny eggs repose. Similar paperweights
were sold having one white pig instead of three. Being the work
of an individual workman, no two specimens are apt to be alike.
Another style contains a simple background of flowers, much like
those intended to enhance the attractiveness of the pig paperweights. The coloring of the flowers is mostly red and blue, and
the appearance of dew on the petals is nicely achieved. The latter
was once held to establish indisputably a ripe old age! All the

Plate 104

THESE NEW WEIGHTS ARE MORE ATTRACTIVE THAN A PHOTOGRAPH CAN SHOW.

Plate 105

MODERN CHINESE PAPERWEIGHTS.

Plate 106

AMERICAN WEIGHT AT TOP. DATED ENGLISH WEIGHT IN CENTER.
CHINESE AT BOTTOM. ALL ARE NEW.

Plate 107
MODERN PAPERWEIGHTS.

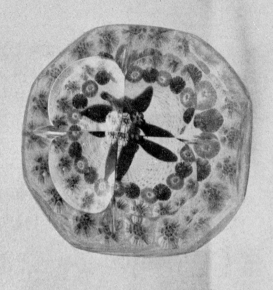

Plate 108

MODERN PAPERWEIGHTS. THE ONE AT RIGHT HAS INTERLACED BACKGROUND

Plate 109

MODERN PAPERWEIGHTS.

Plate 110

MODERN "THREE PIGS" AND "THREE BIRDS" PAPERWEIGHTS.

paperweights of this type are large and weigh from three to four pounds.

In the fall of 1937 these weights were being widely peddled. At an antiques exhibit in New York that year one weight containing three pigs was sold at $30.00 and another with a single pig was disposed of at $35.00. I have seen them priced as high as $150.00 by reputable dealers who honestly believed them to be old. It is such "unique" pieces which trip veteran collectors who probably would easily spot copies of old and well-known designs.

Another paperweight, which is so similar in style to those illustrated as to appear to have come from the same glassworker, has a cluster of strawberries and flowers in the center. These strawberry weights are of the same size as the others and also weigh from three to three and one-half pounds each. One of them was on display at an antiques show in 1937. It had been sold to a dealer at $60.00, along with a tale of how the seller had been trying to buy it for years and had just succeeded in prying it loose from the stubborn owner! One of the New England glass companies did produce strawberry weights but these exhibit finer workmanship and are not nearly as large as the copies.

During the late 1930's, an attempt was made to reproduce the New England Pear paperweight. The result was a far cry from the genuine article, either in coloring or workmanship.

The Spanish proverb which advises suffering wives that it is better to put up with the devil you know than take on the angel you don't, may be applied to paperweights. Collectors would do well to realize that they cannot become connoisseurs of paperweights by reading articles or looking at photographs. They should learn to appreciate fine workmanship so as to tell the good from the poor at a glance. Learn to know glass by the quality of the metal and the design and coloring by their artistic excellence. Look out for dated pieces in which the year can be read too easily. As his education in antiques progresses, the amateur will be impressed by the number of collector's "Don'ts!" that he must remember.

Chapter IX

LAMPS AND GLOBES

There has always been a demand for lamps and there probably always will be. The overlay types in particular have long been popular. The name comes from the fact that they are so-called "case" glass, which is made in two or sometimes three parts. A lamp bowl may be opaque-white on the outside and a clear jade-green on the inside. When cut through, allowing the color to be seen by way of the various cuttings, an attractive effect is obtained. In the old days this glass was expensive to make so these lamps never were very cheap. About twenty-five years ago, overlay lamp bowls were imported from Czechoslovakia which could be set in either modern or old bases. The complete lamps also came here via the same route. Apparently it was cheaper to obtain the glassware from the Czechs than it was to make it on our own shores. Naturally, those lamps with cut stems as well as bowls cost a great deal more. On Plate 111 may be seen some of the new lamps that were marketed years ago. On the same page are wall sconces which were sold during the same period and also one style of peg-lamp.

Lamps in the old Sandwich heart pattern were reproduced during the 1920's in clear glass, green, amethyst, pink and possibly other colors. They looked new. One is illustrated on Plate 112 along with a pair of reproductions of an earlier style of Sandwich lamp. The latter are very good copies and might deceive even careful buyers unless they were studied with extreme care. All the genuine old lamp collars of the period are of either brass or pewter. On this pair of lamps the collars are treated to resemble discolored old brass. If the lamps *were* really old the bases would have *some* resonance when struck, even if only a little, because the glass is too thick to ring clearly. If you struck one of those in the illustration, you would hear that dead thud one soon learns to associate with all the reproductions now on the market.

On Plate 113 are two other styles of lamps which have been on sale for some years. The one on the left at first was made in clear glass only. Later copies were made in color.

Six types of the new varieties that are selling today are shown on Plates 114 and 115. These range in height from nine to fourteen inches. Those with the engraved deer, as well as the smaller Grape pattern, are after the manner of the old ruby Bohemian glass. Stems and bases have the "antique finish." The lamp with the leaf pattern bowl (Plate 115), which was a favorite design at Sandwich, can be obtained in either clear glass or with a frosted finish. Doubtless these have also been made with colored bowls.

The overlay lamp at the left in the upper row of Plate 114 is in amethyst, cut to clear, and is quite beautiful. The other overlay lamp on the same page is made in blue or ruby, over crystal. All these are sold by the maker frankly as reproductions. The harm they do is when they find their way into antique shops to be sold at the high figures commanded by old ones. Another new marble-base lamp on the market carries a round bowl in Inverted Thumbprint.

During the early 1940's, a "miniature night lamp" appeared on the market, in the Moon and Star pattern. The listing of this pattern in my *Early American Pressed Glass* may be considered quite complete because it was taken from a catalogue of the makers, Adams & Co., of Pittsburgh. This catalogue does not mention miniature night lamps. Upon examination, it is found that the so-called miniature lamp has been formed from the reproduction Moon and Star eggcup mold.

The lamp is three and one-half inches high and two and three-quarters inches wide at the widest part. The footed base is two and one-half inches wide. The glass opening at the top, where the brass collar is cemented on, is barely wide enough to insert a lead pencil. The brass collar and burner of one such lamp has been corroded by the use of some solution or acid to give it a greenish or "antique" appearance. The wick was new, freshly kerosened

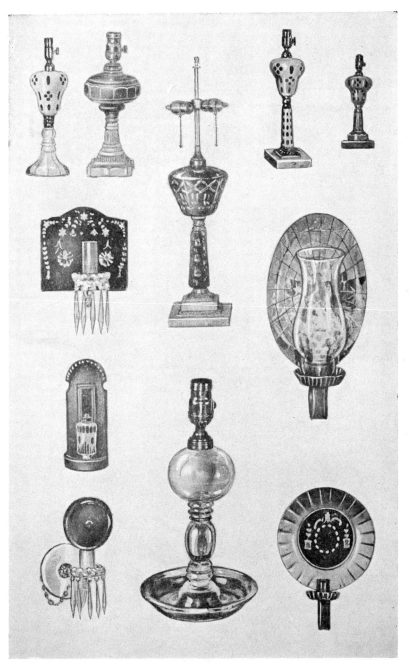

Plate 111
LAMPS AND WALL SCONCES AS PRESENTED TWENTY-FIVE
OR MORE YEARS AGO.

Plate 112

REPRODUCTIONS OF EARLY SANDWICH GLASS LAMPS.

Plate 113
THERE ARE MANY STYLES OF NEW HURRICANE GLOBES,
AS WELL AS LAMPS AND SHADES.

Plate 114
MODERN OVERLAY COLORED LAMPS.

Plate 115

CANDLESTICKS.

SANDWICH STYLE LAMP.   OVERLAY LAMP.

Plate 116

WESTWARD-HO LAMP CONVERTED FROM NEW GOBLET MOLD.

Plate 117

REPRODUCTION OF EARLY SANDWICH LAMP IN OPAQUE
JADE-GREEN AND TRANSLUCENT WHITE.

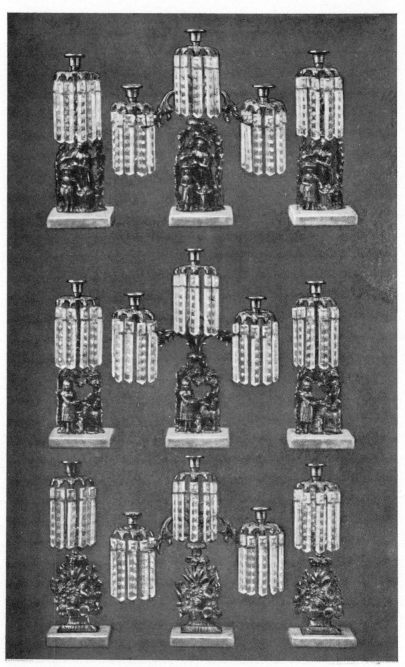

Plate 118
THREE DESIGNS IN NEW GIRANDOLES.

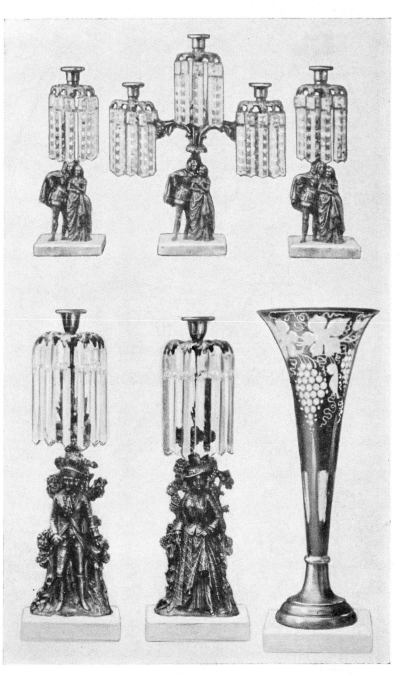

Plate 119
GIRANDOLES AND OVERLAY VASE.

Plate 120

NEW HANGING LAMPS.

Plate 121

NEW LAMP GLOBES.

and had been lighted at least once. Traces of what looked like fresh plaster of Paris could be seen around the brass collar. The same style collars, burners and glass chimneys have been on sale by a house carrying many reproductions in the Midwest! The base of the lamp had also been ground to simulate wear. Such a lamp is not a reproduction, because it was never made in the old glass. Even so, they are being sold to collectors as old and advertised at $6.50, $7.50 and $10.00. Lately a new Moon and Star miniature night lamp was seen in amber, complete with a matching amber shade, also in the Moon and Star pattern.

At the time when our markets were being flooded with West-ward-Ho goblets and sauce dishes, a new lamp was made from the goblet mold. The counterfeits were planted in the deep South, but evidently were not made in quantity since they have not been seen in the East. Plate 116.

Not long ago an early Sandwich lamp was sent to me for examination. It was obviously new, and bore marks of carefully applied "age" designed to deceive the purchaser. The lamp is pictured on Plate 117. It is eleven and three-quarters inches high and is merely an improved model of the one shown in the lower left-hand corner of Plate 113. The opaque-white in the square base and pedestal is an unpleasant yellowish-white. The opaque-green in the bowl is also off-shade. The collar has been dented in, presumably by a hammer, in such a manner as to give a realistic appearance of age. The collar also has been treated with a solution which contributes to its antique appearance. The same copy has appeared in several different color combinations.

During the past five years, which saw the end of wartime shortages, certain manufacturers have been expanding their facilities and as a consequence, almost every conceivable type of novelty lamp is now being displayed in department stores and gift shops. Not a few are also in antique shops. These lamps run the gamut from late Victorian "Gone with the Winds" to miniature night lamps. Some of these are described in Chapter XVI, concerning novelties.

A number of years ago there was a great interest in girandoles, but that interest died out and a good many dealers took losses when their popularity waned. Old-timers remember the day when brass candlesticks were in great demand and dealers and collectors were forever on the watch against copies but today no one thinks about the reproductions, for collectors seldom ask even for originals. On Plates 115, 118 and 119 are shown candlesticks and girandoles as they were presented during the 1920's and 1930's. Good old ones were of fine French gilt but most of the newly made sets are of brass ready to receive an "antique finish" intended to stimulate interest in collectors. A few patterns besides those shown are also made.

Hanging lamps, particularly for halls, are in great demand by home builders. They have always been a scarce item. On Plate 120 are shown many styles of new ones which have been sold in New England. The bowls were advertised as hand blown and hand cut, and apparently great care was given to secure correctness of design and workmanship. They may in time become good antiques.

Fitting out lamps has always been a problem because it is often well-nigh impossible to find the proper globe to fit. Various manufacturers have been making copies for years. On Plate 113 are two styles which have been on the market for at least fifteen years. They were made for the old-style astral lamps, because the fine old shades broke so often. On the same plate is shown a hurricane globe. Many new ones are made now, one of the most attractive having an eagle engraved on it.

Some years ago I was in an antique shop in Philadelphia, discussing reproductions with a dealer who has watched them with more than usual care for many years, both here and abroad. He said a woman came in to his shop not long ago, and asked about a pair of old hurricane globes. When she heard the price she nearly swooned, for it was several times more than she had paid for some a short time before. She told him he was a highway robber and, in the course of the conversation, described her magnificent globes with eagles on them. "Would you care to tell me what you paid for them?" the dealer asked politely. "I paid," said the customer, "seventy-five dollars." "Would you like me to sell you a pair exactly like them for thirty dollars?" he asked again. She told him she would not. She was quite content with her bargain.

Plate 121 shows a dozen different types of new lamp shades which have been on the market for at least twelve years, but for these you should not pay the price of old ones!

Chapter X

BOHEMIAN GLASS

At various intervals since collecting American antiques became the fashionable fad in this young country of ours, there have been revivals of interest in Bohemian glass. Upon hearing the name, the average collector immediately conjures up a vision of a ruby-red glass with grapevines and bunches of grapes etched or engraved in a frosted effect against the red background. Various sorts of ruby-red glass were made at our own factories but since the earliest ware was all imported, the trade and the public gave it the generic title of Bohemian glass.

As a matter of fact, glassmaking was an important industry in Bohemia for several centuries. Many kinds and types of glass were produced, both blown and pressed. Bohemian cut glass was famous the world over. The varieties the average collector knows best today are those illustrated in this book. During the 1870's and 1880's, such huge shipments of all their specialties, including engraved, cut, gilded, painted, etc., came into this country, that quantities of it survived for us to collect years later. Many of the articles shipped in were of an ornamental character, and did not suffer the hard usage of tableware. To judge between the old and the new is largely a matter of appreciating quality, workmanship, and preservation.

Twenty-five or thirty years ago Bohemian glass again became very popular, particularly the ruby-red pieces. The vogue was so great that the supply was reduced until it became quite scarce. Naturally, the finest pieces available went into collectors' cabinets, as permanent tenants.

As was to be expected, a flood of reproductions came from Bohemia, now Czechoslovakia. Some were quite beautiful and others very crude. Commercialism knows no geographical boundaries.

One of the earliest reproductions brought to my notice was the little pinch-bottle cordial set, shown in the lower right-hand corner of Plate 123. These were displayed in amber as well as in ruby, all with the etched grapevine. About the same time there appeared two different styles of vases, eleven inches high, which were an opaque-red over milk-white, with a design after "Eggermann." These are illustrated at the top of Plate 124.

Shortly thereafter the ruby glass engraved with the ever-popular stag or hunting scenes, as well as the Vintage or Grapevine patterns, arrived in large quantities. They were decorative and well worth the prices asked by department stores, but no one should think of paying the values set on them when offered as genuine antiques.

On Plate 122 are shown a number of the finer pieces, engraved with the Stag. At the top of this page is shown a console set which came in sapphire blue, amethyst, green, and ruby. The jar in the center of the page is twelve inches high and was made in blue as well as in ruby. The one on the left of the center is fourteen inches high and may be found in blue, amber, green, and ruby. The one on the right is ten inches high and is obtainable in green, blue, and ruby. In the lower corner is one eleven inches high which was sold in blue, amber, and ruby. It will be noted that these are all fairly large pieces that create handsome color effects in any home. The bowl in the center of the page is greatly reduced in size in the picture. It is an eight-and-a-half-inch size, four inches deep. It was made in ruby only, as far as I can learn.

The covered jar and large vase in the center of Plate 124 were still being made and sold in 1938. The jar is eight inches high and comes in crystal, in blue, and in ruby. The vase is seven and one-half inches high and is found in blue, and in ruby. The large candlestick pictured on the same page is eleven inches high. This was still on sale during the 1930's though it was carried over a number of years. I recall a similar pair of candlesticks that were brought to me about twenty-five years ago, by a newly married

Plate 122
ARRAY OF BOHEMIAN ENGRAVED PIECES.

Plate 123

RUBY BOHEMIAN WINE AND LIQUEUR SETS, IMPORTED DURING
PAST THIRTY YEARS.

Plate 124
ENGRAVED RUBY BOHEMIAN GLASS.
Note the two different styles of candlesticks.

Plate 125

FINER ENGRAVED PIECES, NOT SEEN SO FREQUENTLY AS THE
TABLE SET IN THE CENTER.

Plate 126
IMPORTED RUBY BOHEMIAN GLASS,
WHICH HAS BEEN WIDELY DISTRIBUTED,

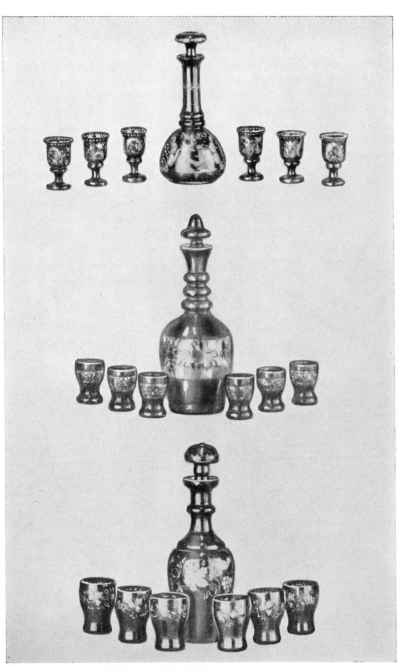

Plate 127
RUBY BOHEMIAN CORDIAL AND LIQUEUR SETS.

young chap who said he had purchased them in an antique shop in
New York State, where he was told they had been bought by the
dealer from a very old lady who wept because she had to part with
family heirlooms, but she had to have coal. It was a familiar story.
He asked me to tell him what I thought of them, which was not
pleasant, because I had to tell him they were not old. He asked me
how I knew, and I showed him the utter absence of any marks of
age. He was still unconvinced, so I finally told him where he
could buy new ones in New York to match exactly those in his
possession. A few weeks later, he came back to tell me I was right.
He had been at the importers' showrooms, and saw his candlesticks
there. He had given them to his wife for Christmas, and unfortunately he had made quite a financial sacrifice to acquire them
because she liked them so much.

The wine set at the left side of the upper part of Plate 123 is
from the old line which came to this country years ago, in ruby,
green, and blue. The liqueur set next to it was made in blue and
ruby only. The liqueur set below it, on the right, came in four
colors—blue, ruby, amber, and green. Next to it, in the center, is
another liqueur set, also from the older line, in amber and ruby and
is engraved in typical Bohemian style, which is attractive enough
to make it popular.

The two large decanters and the wine glass shown in the lower
part of Plate 123 are fine examples of the style of glass that was
imported about twenty-five years ago by a New York importing
firm. The set included a large service plate, nine inches in diameter; a salad plate in a seven-inch size, goblets, wines, cordials,
salts, and finger bowls in two sizes. A large line is still carried
today, as shown on Plate 126. It will be noted that the wines are
offered with the round bowl, as well as with the cylindrical shape.
This present-day work is crude, and in no way compares with that
workmanship for which there was an active market when pocketbooks were fatter. The compotes on Plate 125 are examples of
that finer workmanship. The one at the top of the page comes in
ruby, amber, and blue.

On Plate 127 are shown three cordial sets. The one at the top of the page is by far the most attractive. It sold at only $6.00 per set of decanter and six glasses. The other two sets were cheaply made for wide distribution and cost $3.75 per set.

The importers of most of this new red Bohemian glass frankly sell it as new. Their business is largely with department stores, gift shops and ceramic studios. If any of these wares find a way into antique shops and are there sold as "genuine antiques," the importers should not be blamed, even though some jobbers in advertisements stress the close resemblance to old models. The major differences between the old and the new Bohemian glass are found in the quality of the workmanship and of the glass itself and in the absence of the usual recognizable signs of age.

So much overlay glass has been imported from Czechoslovakia that some collectors ignore the fact that it was also made in other countries. Many of our own factories produced an excellent quality of this popular glass, but never to the extent of the European sources. Importing houses today have very beautiful "case glass" pieces, such as those illustrated on Plate 147. This glass is made in two parts. After a piece is completed, it is cut and, in some cases, enameled in floral designs in colors or covered with a delicate tracery in gold. "Lusters," vases and covered jars were favorites. In overlay glass, we made chiefly lamps and utilitarian items and seldom attempted to match the elaborate pieces, so many of which came from Czechoslovakia. European countries concentrated largely on ornamental and decorative objects.

Chapter XI

DOLPHIN CANDLESTICKS AND COMPOTES

Among the earliest items to be sought eagerly by collectors before the great vogue developed for either blown or pressed glass were candlesticks, particularly those known as "dolphin." Since the demand was great and the supply limited, reproductions duly followed. Genuine dolphin candlesticks were made both early and late, but it is as easy to differentiate their periods as it is to date costumes. While adequate documentary proof is not available, it is safe to assume that the first specimens of this variety were produced by the Boston & Sandwich Glass Company, perhaps as early as the 1830's, certainly during the 1840's. We have also never hesitated to believe that the first to appear on the market were those with the large, single square base. They are larger, heavier and are found more often in the soft, delicate opaque shades which were more in favor at Sandwich than at any other glassworks.

Next in importance and almost of the same period are those with a double square base. This style was reproduced many years ago and was still being made prior to World War II. As far as I could ever learn, none of the reproductions originated in this country but were brought here from Czechoslovakia, largely through a New York importing house. The Pittsburgh type of dolphin candlestick with a hexagonal base has been reproduced in this country in milk-white, though the earliest copy was produced in Bohemia many years ago in sapphire blue, through the efforts of a New England antique dealer.

Illustrated on Plate 128 are an old and a new dolphin candlestick, the reproduction being at the right. Significant differences may be quickly noted. The genuine dolphin is smaller, the glass is a finer quality of metal, the petals are larger, thicker, and tip slightly over at the top. The new one appears to be made of com-

237

mon window glass. The petals are short and are tilted upward. The old candlestick is ten inches tall, and the new one, ten and one-half inches.

There would be more difficulty in judging the genuine from the spurious, especially for the amateur, in the variety with the double-step base than any of the others, because the old ones were made from different molds at different periods. Even so, the student can always detect the reproductions with a little careful study. Years ago, collectors judged by the misalignment of a seam in the paneled top with the seam in the tail. Early dolphin candlesticks were made in two sections and fused together, thus they were often slightly uneven, and the panel seam in the top was hardly ever in line with the center of the seam in the tail.

On the new ones, the seams were always perfectly centered because they were made in a one-piece mold. Later, very clever copies of the old double-step type were made that eliminated the telltale irregularities. They were turned out in crystal, milk-white, and in combinations of opaque shades, such as white tops and jade green bases, or all green or blue and white, in all of which the makers of these reproductions took care to have the seams vary. The only way one could tell the old from the new was to compare the finer details. There are some old dolphin candlesticks in which the petal tops are not as thick as those pictured, and do not tip downward as much, but there are no genuine old ones with petals as thin or tilted upward as sharply as the new one pictured here. A good many of the earliest dolphins were fused together with the addition of a thin wafer of glass. This method was later discarded, and genuine old ones may be found without this wedge-like piece connecting the two parts.

The candlestick on the left of Plate 129 was made on special order for a New England dealer over thirty years ago. This dealer sent a fragment of sapphire blue Sandwich glass to Austria (so the story goes), but it was more likely Bohemia, then a part of Austria-Hungary, so that the right color might be obtained. The new candlesticks may be detected by the quality of the glass and the sharpness of details, especially in the fins on the fish. The candle-

Plate 128

OLD AND NEW DOLPHIN CANDLESTICKS. THE FAKE IS ON THE RIGHT.

stick at the right in the same illustration is a genuine old one, pictured so that the soft details in the dolphin may be compared with the counterfeit. Dolphin candlesticks having the hexagonal base are not a Sandwich product but were made in the Pittsburgh area, probably during the 1850's. Many copies are seen of this Pittsburgh type that have been made in this country. They are usually seen in milk-white, though they have been advertised in yellow also, and average from nine to nine and one-half inches in height. This style may also be found in a four-inch size.

Plate 129
OLD AND NEW DOLPHIN CANDLESTICK. AN ORIGINAL IS ON THE RIGHT.

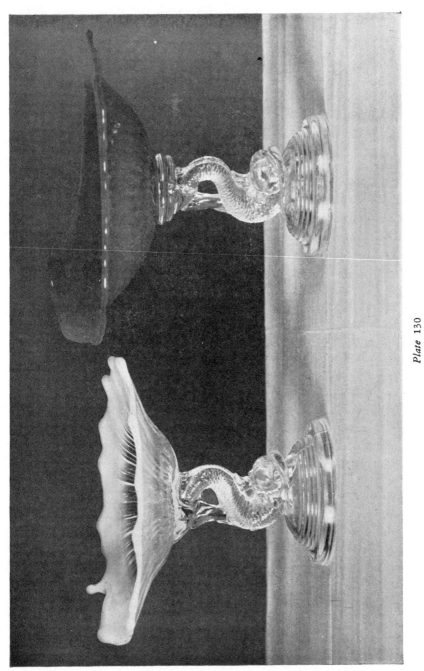

Plate 130

OLD AND NEW DOLPHIN COMPOTE. THE FAKE IS ON THE RIGHT.

Gift shop items in the way of modern dolphin candlesticks which are not a copy of any early type confuse many dealers and collectors. They are now old enough so that families who own them say they "can always remember them," or "these came to me from Aunt Harriet." They are anywhere from thirty to thirty-five years old. This type has a round base carrying a diamond pattern, a husky short dolphin and a ribbed socket. They are found in a bright sapphire blue, amber, and probably other colors.

Another strictly modern dolphin candlestick is nine inches tall and has a double-square base, the upper square being quite low in height. The dolphin is mounted on a round pedestal on this second step. These have been out for only a few years and should not deceive any buyer.

Popular collectibles during the 1920's were the dolphin compotes together with the matching so-called "petticoat dolphin" candlesticks. They had decorative appeal and lent themselves admirably to interesting dining table arrangements. Four of the candlesticks and a pair of compotes completed a picture. They could be found readily in the days before the vogue for pattern glass swept the country. The color range included clear to opalescent, yellow-opalescent, blue-opalescent, and a greenish-peacock shade, the last named being the rarest. Today the candlesticks are difficult to find since they are largely in the hands of collectors. Reproductions of the compotes have been on the market for a number of years. Pictured are an old and a new one, the copy being at the left. Differences between them are obvious when shown side by side. Plate 130.

This style of dolphin compote was never made originally in the color combinations of the new one. The base of the copy pictured is in clear glass and the bowl, opaque-blue. As may be clearly seen, the bowl is larger and attached to the base by two wafers of glass. The old dish was made all in one piece. Other similar reproductions have been seen in curious combinations of colors, such as an opaque-blue bowl and an opaque-cream, or coffee-colored base. These new compotes should never deceive anyone again, after a careful study is made of the accompanying photograph. No reproductions of the petticoat dolphin candlesticks have ever appeared that are worthy of mention.

A style of dolphin compote which should mislead no one is one which has an extra large bowl, weighing down the dolphin, usually seen in milk-white, though sometimes in color. The older of these, which has been on the market for ten or fifteen years, has a deep shell-shaped bowl. The newer type is found in two sizes, seven and eleven inches, and has a dolphin on a hexagonal base supporting a large round bowl. Neither is a copy of an old compote. They are strictly modern, but seem to fool new dealers and collectors.

Chapter XII

FAKED AMERICAN SILVER

By JOHN MARSHALL PHILLIPS

Caveat emptor should be the creed of the American silver collector, who, as a fledgling in his quest for the fine and rare, is apt to prove easy prey for the faker. It is in the spirit of service that the following hints are offered to the would-be collector with the hope that he may spare his purse as well as defend the honor of American craftsmanship in the precious metal.

In buying silver the following points should be carefully considered: (1) source, (2) style, (3) workmanship, and (4) marks. The first of these, while bearing least weight in the final analysis, is worthy of consideration. It is most comforting to acquire a piece that has descended in proper custody or one that has been vetted by a reputable dealer, but even these considerations should not dull the would-be purchaser's sense with regard to the other requirements for vetting.

The importance of style cannot be overemphasized, for it is as art historian and artist that the faker tends to fail most conspicuously. Fortunately sufficient silver has survived to enable us to trace with a fair degree of accuracy the evolution of design and decoration. With such knowledge it is fairly easy to date a piece within ten years of its making. One having such knowledge would be wary of the teapot illustrated here (Plates 131 and 132), of a type prevalent in Europe about 1750, which bears a crude attempt at the stamp of the Bostonian, John Coney, who died in 1722! For information on the evolution of forms in American silver, one should consult C. Louise Avery's excellent catalogue of the Clearwater Collection (Metropolitan Museum of Art) as well as her treatise on style in *Early American Silver*. E. Alfred Jones's *Old*

Plate 131

TEAPOT PURPORTING TO BE BY JOHN CONEY (1655–1722).

Silver of Europe and America and the author's *American Silver* might also be consulted.

Closely related to style and more subtle than the silversmith's mark is the criterion of workmanship, which can be measured only after an exhaustive study of the known work of a given man. For the artists in metal, just as the artists in other media, have their definite peculiarities which proclaim the man. These may be found either in the hammerwork, moldings, method of soldering, or peculiar use of some form of decoration which runs through their work

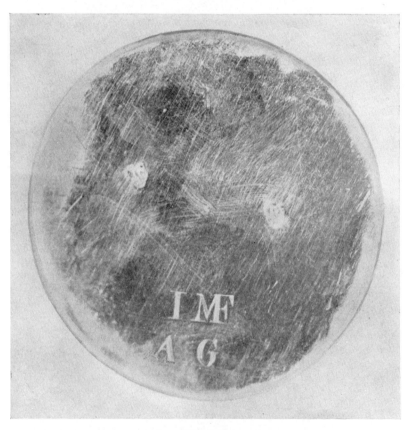

Plate 132
BASE OF TEAPOT SHOWING CRUDE ATTEMPTS AT
FORGING CONEY'S STAMP.

On the beaker: *Robbert Sandersen* 1685

Plate 133

GENUINE BEAKER MADE IN 1685 BY CORNELIS VANDERBURCH.

Plate 134

DUTCH BEAKER, 1686, BEARING A FORGED STAMP OF VANDERBURCH'S.
The poor quality of the engraving when compared with the Sanders Beaker, caused intensive study.

Plate 135

ENGLISH BEAKER BEARING A FORGED MARK OF
JOHN BURT'S ON THE SIDE.

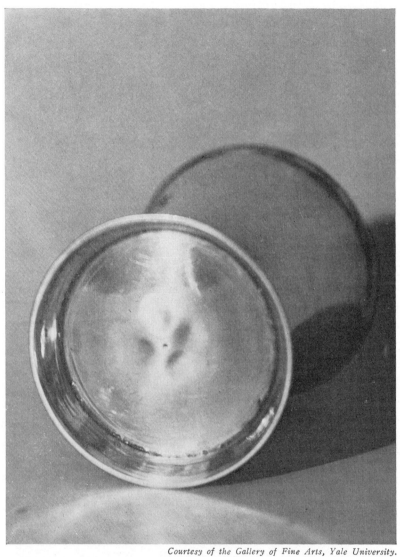

Plate 136

THE BASE OF THE FORGED BURT BEAKER SHOWING BRUISES WHERE
HALLMARKS HAVE BEEN ERASED.

either in plastic decoration or engraved design. An example of this is seen in the famous Sanders beaker by Vanderburch (Plate 133) and an old Dutch beaker bearing a spurious stamp, purporting to be the work of Cornelis Vanderburch of New York, who was known to have been working in the last two decades of the seventeenth century (Plate 134). The small beaker bearing the contemporary date 1686 made its debut into the world of American silver in 1929 and was acclaimed by the connoisseurs as a fine example of this rare maker's work, despite the fact that the pieces in company with it were rejected as obvious fakes. It was not until the acquisition of the Sanders beaker, dated 1685, for the Garvan Collection in 1932, that the fraud was discovered. A careful comparison of the engraving and hammerwork prompted a searching study of the mark. If the buyer is within reach of a municipal museum fortunate enough to have a collection of silver, it would be well to compare the tentative acquisition with a known piece for the master's touch.

I once saw a coffeepot of a type found only in Philadelphia and Baltimore c. 1790–1810, bearing a stamp REVERE for the famous Boston craftsman. It was engraved with a coat of arms of a style popular in 1765–80, which had been copied from a known bookplate engraved by Revere.

There remains for consideration the silversmith's mark, which should be noted most carefully. One may find a forged mark on a newly made piece of silver which is easy to detect from weight, the uniform scratches simulating wear, and the engraving. More difficult is the forged stamp on an old originally unmarked piece or an old mark cut from a spoon and carefully inserted in a larger and more valuable piece. The latter is usually discernible under a strong glass, having a peculiar color around the inlay of the solder. In the case of the former, one should be careful to note the surface surrounding the punch to ascertain whether or not it has been bruised, as is the case in the process of recent stamping, which once noted, is easily recognized. One should also be on the lookout for erased marks. The beaker illustrated (Plates 135 and 136), of a style as yet not noted as American, bears on its side a spurious mark of John Burt and upon its base the bruises where the four English hallmarks had been erased. Again let me urge a comparison of the mark with known examples above suspicion in the collections of credited museums. It was the wish of the late Francis P. Garvan, in giving the Mabel Brady Garvan Collection to Yale, to establish at Yale University a bureau of standards where a prospective buyer could submit his proposed purchase for comparison with the pieces in that great collection.

In closing let me urge you to give careful consideration to pieces by the following silversmiths whose forged marks have been frequently noted: Pygan Adams, Thauvet Besly, John Brevoort, Zacariah Brigden, Benjamin and John Burt, John Coney, William Cowell, John Dixwell, John Edwards, Daniel Henchman, Jacob Hurd, Knight Leverett, Myer Myers, John Noyes, Gerrit Onckelbag, Paul Revere, Joseph Richardson, George Ridout, Thomas Shields, Simeon Soumain, Philip Syng, Koenradt Ten Eyck, Andrew Tyler, Jacobus Van der Spiegel, Bancroft Woodcock and Benjamin Wynkoop.

Chapter XIII

CERAMICS

It is not possible in this volume to expatiate fully upon all the reproductions of the various lines that fall properly under the heading of ceramics. My particular province being glass, I have not had occasion to devote much study to pottery and porcelain. All I shall attempt is to describe those fakes which are most frequently found in shops and are sometimes offered for sale as genuinely old ware.

On Plate 137 are pictured three tea sets in pink luster, showing different adaptations of the ever-popular House pattern. All three have been on the market for the past twenty or twenty-five years. None shows the quality or the feeling of the originals. Many new articles may have an appearance of age until placed next to the really old.

On Plate 138 in the bottom row is what is described as "Sunderland Lustre Liverpool jugs." The black decoration consists of the "ship-wright arms" on one side, an old clipper ship on the reverse, with a coat of arms lettered JAMES LEECH in front. These were made in three sizes. A critical examination of the ware itself would disclose its newness. The price to the trade was from $3.00 to $4.00, according to size.

In the center of the same illustration are pictured some new examples of silver resist, though these are now about thirty-five years of age. The tea set at the top of the page is "the very best Carlsbad China" in the "early American silver resist Berry decoration." It is attractive enough, but true silver resist is difficult to reproduce. In the first place, the old ware is delicate, usually very light in weight, and the resist is applied differently. While this does not always tell the complete story it is, nevertheless, one way to judge. Most copies of both silver and copper luster are much heavier than the old and the copyist is seldom careful as to the correct shapes. A student can easily detect the differences. Cups and saucers were made in the same Berry pattern in gold luster, but they are too new looking to deceive anyone. The makers were not thinking of deception, but of meeting a popular demand at low prices. On Plate 139 are shown some new English copper luster pieces which came in through Canada about ten years ago. The two pieces on the left are very heavy. I have seen numerous other pieces to match in shops, including a teapot and a creamer.

Dealers in ceramics as well as collectors had reason to complain during the early 1930's, at the flood of imitations in Wedgwood coming into this country from Germany and Japan. You see them in certain antique shops as well as in many department stores and gift shops. A number of years ago an importer who carried an extensive line of them sent out circulars in which it was stated that "Wedgwood" was merely a generic item for that class of ware. He advertised his importations as "Wedgewood" (note an extra *e* inserted in the name) whereupon the New York agents of the famous firm of Josiah Wedgwood & Sons, at the head of which is a direct descendant of the founder, took legal steps in the matter and obtained an injunction to prevent the misuse of the name. This action was not contested, and the importer was compelled to find another designation for the imitations. The Japanese product also was stopped from being offered as "Wedgwood." The MADE IN GERMANY or MADE IN JAPAN is often scraped out or stamped over with the dealer's name, when found in certain antique dealers' shops.

Real Wedgwood has been plainly marked with the maker's name uninterruptedly ever since 1769. In making the genuine a quite different technique is used. The blue body of the piece was made first, and the white cameo decorations applied afterward. This called for a high degree of skill. Modern practice has modified the method. The cheaper grades of imitations are made in one piece in white, medallions and all, and the blue slip is applied where needed. Another line of this ware, but better executed, is

Plate 137

THREE DIFFERENT PINK LUSTER TEA SETS IN THE HOUSE PATTERN.

Plate 138
GOLD AND SILVER RESIST. SUNDERLAND LUSTER LIVERPOOL JUG.

Plate 139

MODERN COPPER LUSTER.

Plate 140

WEDGWOOD STYLE PORCELAIN IMITATIONS.

illustrated on Plate 140. It is naturally much less expensive than the authentic. The inferior quality of the workmanship is plainly apparent and is the most reliable criterion. You can see partly obliterated mold marks on the imitation which shows that the pieces have been pressed and not turned, as the genuine pieces are. Also, it is well to look on the inside of the imitations for indentations which show where the cameo decorations were impressed on the outside. Today reputable dealers will not, and the unscrupulous dare not, offer for sale as Wedgwood what is not Wedgwood.

An importer brought over quite an extensive line of small Staffordshire animals about twelve years ago. Some of these are illustrated on Plate 141. The figure on the left in each case is a genuine old one. The new almost all carry the Chelsea gold anchor mark. There is no extra charge for the anchor marks, which is the first thing the inexperienced collector looks for as a proof of age and authenticity. On the genuine, the anchor mark is underneath the glaze, not over it.

All of these imported figures are plainly marked GERMANY in a small ring in the center of the base. Our laws require that the name of the country of origin be so stamped. I have seen some of these with the "Germany" carefully eradicated. In some cases the unscrupulous seller will apply transparent varnish over the rough spot in the glaze caused by the erasure of the betraying mark. All these new imports are very bright and shining. The gold bands about the bases also are too bright. Note how worn and soft looking the gold stripes appear on the base of the goat at the left on Plate 141. Often the pottery is yellower in the old ones, a sign of respectable age.

On Plates 142, 143, 144, 145, and 146 may be noted imported copies of Staffordshire animals and figurines which have been on the market for about twenty-seven years. On most of these the coloring is brighter and harsher. The paste never looks like the old. My considered advice to the new collector is to study carefully old specimens before going far afield. The new anchor-marked specimens will not give much trouble, but the older reproductions, without new marks, require closer scrutiny. The small pebbled poodle pictured is an excellent copy. In my own collection, which numbers about two thousand, I have just two such dogs and they happen to be a pair—a right and a left. Mine have collars but no locket, and each has a small hole in the base—utilized by the maker while the piece was in the process of drying. A good many of the copies do not have this hole, though some do. It requires an expert to tell the old from new. The faces of the old vary because they were hand decorated. So do the new. Original dogs of this period date between 1840–50.

The squirrel on Plate 146 is an example of an exceedingly poor copy. As in many cases of reproductions, it displays very poor workmanship. The painted face borders on the ludicrous. From the picture, it may be noted that the large flakes of paint have chipped off the lower part of the figure. One could take any sharp object and peel it off. Squirrels have always been among the sought-after animals by collectors, but whoever produced the object illustrated could not hope to fool even a novice.

Also being reproduced are quantities of those quaint little Staffordshire cottage ornaments, which some collectors designate as the "naughty series." Among this group is one entitled, "Return —at one o'clock in the morning"; "The Wedding night"; "The first in bed puts out the lights"; and so forth. The new ones are easily recognized because the script in the title is larger and blacker, whereas in the old ones the lettering was never so large and heavy; it was more like a dainty script. Mention of these new items is made here, so that collectors may know that copies of these cottage genre pottery pieces have been made and are marketed commercially.

On Plate 147 is shown a "Dresden" toilet set and also a shoe. Quite a bit of this bric-a-brac goes to gift shops and is seldom seen in antique shops. Recently, sets of Dresden miniature pieces decorated with forget-me-nots have appeared. These include a settee and two side chairs, a piano, small chair and a sprinkling pot. They average from two and three-quarters to three and one-half inches in height.

Plate 141

STAFFORDSHIRE ANIMALS AND MINIATURE TOBIES. EACH ONE ON THE LEFT IS OLD.

Plate 142
STAFFORDSHIRE GROUPS, ALL IMPORTED.

Plate 143
STAFFORDSHIRE FIGURES, IMPORTED DURING PAST THIRTY YEARS.

Plate 144
STAFFORDSHIRE REPRODUCTIONS.

Plate 145

STAFFORDSHIRE ANIMALS, ALL IMPORTED,

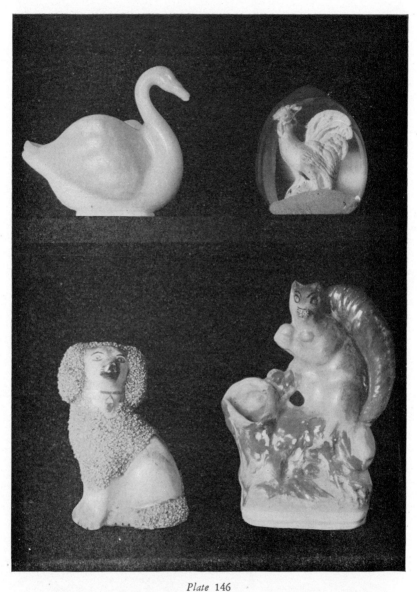

Plate 146

Upper Row: NEW MILK-WHITE SWAN SALT AND A ROOSTER
PAPERWEIGHT FROM CZECHOSLOVAKIA.
Lower Row: TWO FAKE STAFFORDSHIRE ANIMALS.

Plate 147
COPIES OF BEAUTIFUL OVERLAY GLASS IN COLORS.
DRESDEN STYLE TOILET SET AND SHOE.

It should be kept in mind by young collectors that fine china and porcelain have been copied, imitated and faked for a great many years. The earlier the copy the better the quality is apt to be, for being sold contemporaneously with the originals, they had to be well done. It requires an expert, who knows not only the goods but the history of the trade, to tell the difference between certain old original pieces and the reproductions made fifty to seventy-five years ago by skillful artisans who knew nothing of mass production but did excellent work because sound craftsmanship was demanded. Today's makers of reproductions consider the profit and ignore quality. Perhaps they reason that ignorant buyers are more numerous than the well informed.

Chapter XIV

MECHANICAL BANKS, OLD AND NEW

The wonder is not that so many successful business and professional men have of recent years taken to collecting old mechanical cast-iron banks, but that they did not begin long ago. There is a generally ignored sentimental side. With age we begin to walk backward to that past when dreams easily turn into reckless impulses, until experience furnishes safety brakes. You will find that the majority of mechanical bank collectors are grown men, though youth is not immune to the appeal of memory. I used to save pennies. The mechanical comedy of the banks made me laugh and, at the same time, made me richer. It is well to laugh when we make money, and in my day we were assured that "a penny saved is a penny earned." It is not necessary to be a tightwad to believe in Poor Richard's wisdom. After all, the extremely ingenious penny-gulping little machines decidedly reflect the American spirit in sundry ways. Moreover, if whatever you associate with the happy days of your youth imparts a sentimental quality to bank collecting, it is also well to remember that one does not have to belong to the "sixty families" of the United States to be able to indulge in this popular hobby. As in all lines of antiques, there are fairly common banks as well as interesting rarities. The scarcer pieces naturally command high prices.

The road of the bank collector is not without its pitfalls. Reproductions were bound to appear as the fad grew, but these can all be listed. If collectors and dealers will take the trouble to note carefully the differences between the old and the new, there need be no great fear about the reproductions. Those which have been copied are all illustrated here from genuine old banks, with the exception of the Trick Monkey, which is of little importance. The *recasts* are the banks that one must guard against, for it is often difficult to distinguish them, even when placed alongside the originals.

The nomenclature of banks is generally derived from the printed names on them. Thus, the Tabby bank has a cat reclining on an egg, which has a ludicrous chicken's head protruding from one end. The egg-shaped part bears the name TABBY BANK. Some banks are labeled on the front side and some on the reverse; others are not inscribed at all. For the latter, homemade descriptive titles have sprung into general use, just as descriptive titles tagged many a piece of pattern glass before an accurate nomenclature became standardized.

Such banks as the Trick Monkey are about twenty-five years old. They are still being made. Collectors can distinguish the twenty-five-year-old variety by studying the surface, since new paint simply cannot be made to look old by wearing off portions of it; by chipping it off; or by banging up the bank generally. This bank has little value as a collector's item.

So far, the recasting of banks has been very limited due to the amount of work involved. Most of those so far copied have been of the more common variety, and hardly worth the time and energy necessary to do them right. The Paddy and His Pig bank is the best of the old ones copied, in the matter of scarcity and value. Just why such a complicated bank was chosen it is difficult to understand. In the recast specimens, the parts are all heavier and fit together poorly. The paint, instead of being smooth, is pebbly because the casting is rough. There is a smoothness in the feel of old paint and an appearance of age that, to an experienced collector, tells the story. Inexperienced buyers before purchasing a Paddy and His Pig should be sure of the source.

This bank was made in a New England factory and its probable popularity was suggested by the heavy immigration from Ireland. Obviously this bank dates from a time when Irish comedians were in demand. It is said that an Irish society requested that this bank cease to be manufactured, because it constituted an insult to the race. Members did not wish to be associated in the public's mind with pigs. Moreover, Paddy is clutching the animal to the point

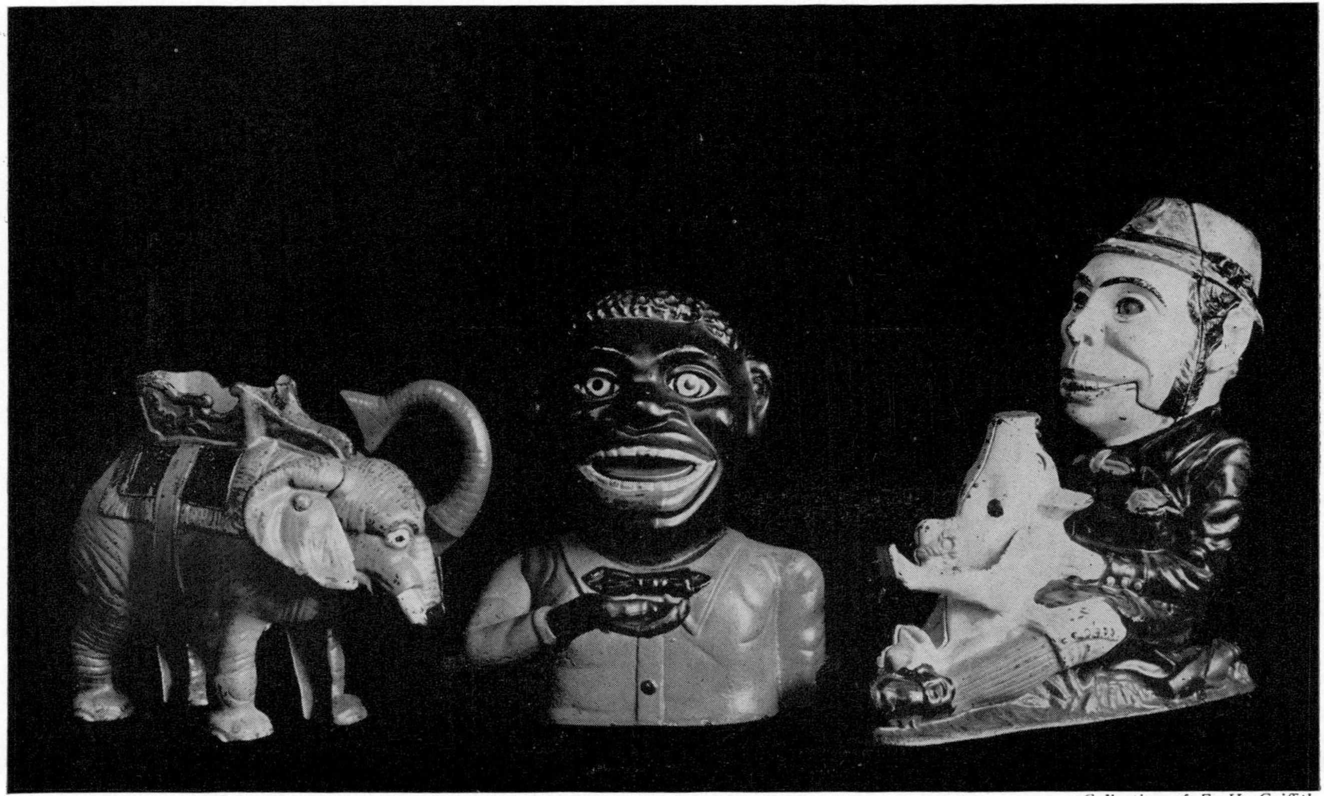

Collection of F. H. Griffith.

Plate 148

TRICK ELEPHANT JOLLY NIGGER. PADDY AND HIS PIG.

Plate 149
FEED THE KITTY.
CAT CHASES MOUSE INTO BUILDING.

Plate 150

TWO VIEWS OF PRESTO SAVINGS BANK.

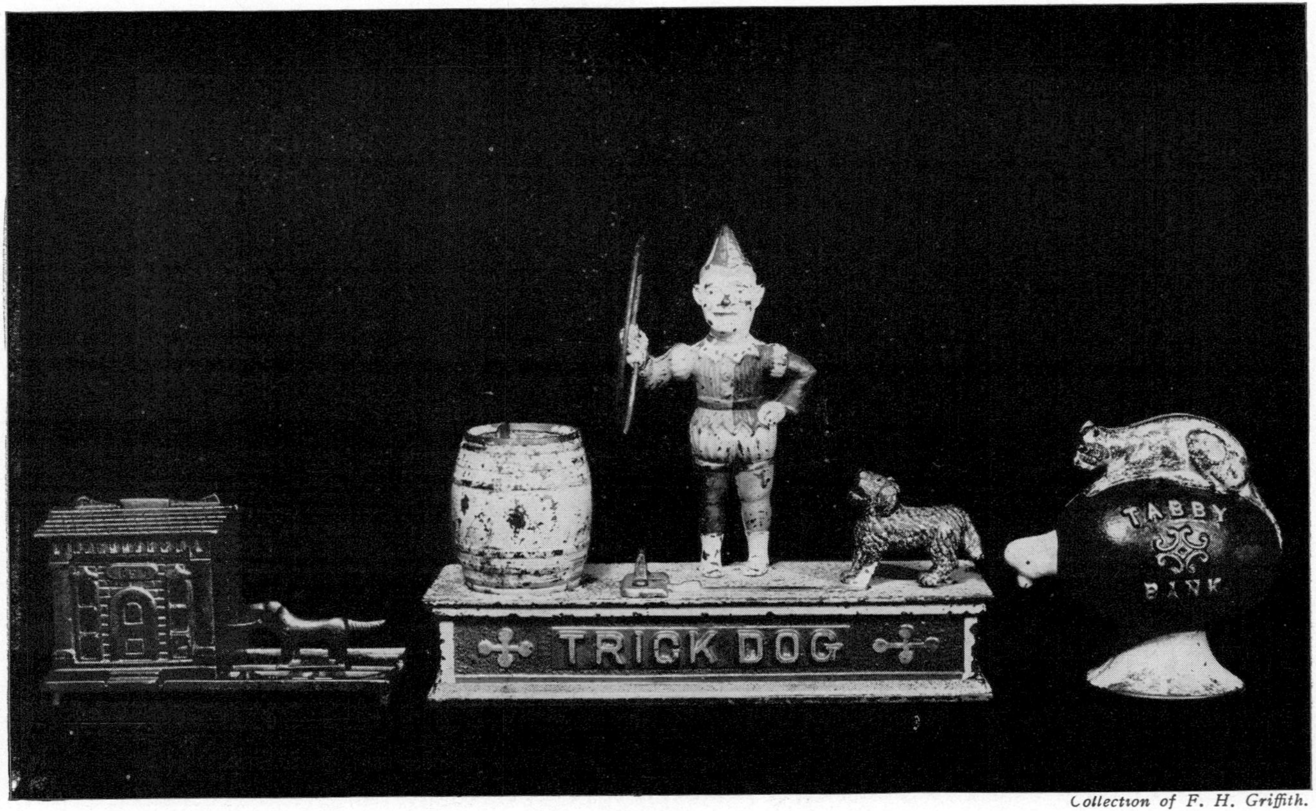

Collection of F. H. Griffith.

Plate 151

THE GEM. TRICK DOG. TABBY BANK.

Plate 152
OWL BANK, ORIGINAL ON LEFT.
BOY AND BULL DOG.   DARKY ON BUCKING MULE.

Plate 153
BULL DOG SAVINGS BANK.
ACTION READY TO TAKE COIN.   RARE ORIGINAL BANK.

Plate 154

SQUIRREL BANK.   TRICK PIG BANK.

of suffocation. Sandy, the Scotchman, might squeeze an asset that tightly—but not an Irishman.

The various difficulties in the matter of recastings are well worth knowing. First, the composition of the cast iron used today is different than in the old banking days. Many malleable castings were used in the old banks; today, nickel has been adapted, which makes the recast banks more brittle and hard.

Most of the iron in the old banks was smooth and soft on the surface. A very fine sand was used and there were many gates on each piece. The fine sand made the casting smooth, whole, and perfect. Today, the sand is coarse and only one gate will be used in pouring a piece. (A gate is the metal ear, or piece, left on the casting when it is taken from the mold.) The gates are later removed or filed smooth on the finished article. In recasting copies of old banks, graphite has been used in an effort to make the casting smooth, but it does not work out successfully.

Since the collecting of old iron mechanical banks has grown in popularity, one might expect many other new ones to come on the market, but it is doubtful if this will happen for several reasons. Today, manufacturers must count on mass production of cheap articles and most of the banks are made up of intricate parts which are not easy to assemble, thereby necessitating considerable labor, which means higher unit cost. During the 1880's and 1890's, when these banks were most popular, labor costs were but a fraction of those prevailing today.

The collection of mechanical banks is fairly well protected against recasts in the case of rarities which go into private collections so quickly that they are never on the market for long. To run across many of the rarest ones in shops would instantly arouse suspicion.

LIST OF FAKE, REMADE AND RECAST BANKS

In the reproducing and faking of mechanical banks there are three classifications to be listed: recast, remade and fakes.

A recast bank is a bank cast from an old original bank. This is assembled, painted, and "antiqued" to make it appear old. An example of a recast bank is the Paddy and His Pig. Some banks have been known to be cast from original patterns and the value of these are the same as any recast or new fake bank. An example of this is the Feed the Kitty bank. Plates 148 and 149.

A remade bank in most cases is a toy or several toy parts assembled with additional new or old parts to make a bank. An example of a remade bank is the Cat Chasing the Mouse into a Building. Plate 149.

Fake banks are banks made by individuals. These were not manufactured by a company for sale to the general public. They are banks that have been made in recent years to sell to collectors only. In most cases they have been "antiqued" to appear old. For example, the Long May It Wave bank and the Carnival bank have paint which is like new but they are represented to be in old original condition.

Another classification could be called "doubtful banks." These are banks that first of all do not look "right." There are no patent papers nor any old catalogue information available to substantiate the manufacture and in all cases they are very poorly made and constructed.

Another way to become suspicious of a bank is to have all known specimens turn up from one source, unless of course patent papers or reliable information can prove the authenticity of the bank.

FAKE BANKS

1. The Forty-Niner Donkey bank—with pack on back. There are two kinds, one a remade and one a fake. The remade "Forty-Niner" was a cigar cutter, the name FORTY-NINER is inscribed on the side. This originally used small steel balls that dropped in the pack and hit mechanism inside, to move either the ears or the tail. It was a gambling item, signifying heads or tails. This cigar cutter was altered to work with pennies and was then called a bank. The other is a fake bank and called "Trick Donkey," this name being on the side. It was cast and a coin slot inserted down the center so that the

coin might fall to the bottom of the base. It is believed to have been made in Providence, Rhode Island.

2. Carnival bank. A figure waving a flag on Boy Scout Camp bank was used to make this bank. It represents a man trying to ring the bell on the usual type of strength-hitting machine. A new fake bank made in Providence, Rhode Island, a few years ago.

3. Long May It Wave bank. Toy cap-shooting cannon, shoots into a parapet. This is a new fake bank made in Providence, Rhode Island, a few years ago. A regular toy cap cannon was utilized in making this bank.

4. Presto bank. A brick building with mouse appearing in the roof when you turn the knob on the side by hand. This is a fake bank made in iron and sheet metal. This bank was originally made by the Crandall Manufacturing Company, who made wood toys. The bank should be wood with brick-like paper pasted on the sides. The mouse springs to the roof as a coin is inserted, which is different from the fake which revolves by hand. Two views of the fake bank are shown. Plate 150.

5. The Jolly Nigger bank. The new one is heavy, rough, operates very poorly and is painted gaudily, though not gaudily enough to cover the pebbly surface. Many recasts in aluminum and iron, easily distinguished as a crude reproduction. Plate 148.

6. Trick Dog bank. The new one has a solid base and is badly painted, whereas the base of the old is composed of four pieces and dated 1888. The name TRICK DOG is cast in the front side of the old one; the new one has this name on top. Plate 151.

7. Trick Elephant bank. A new one of these is more difficult to distinguish than the Trick Dog. Old ones were originally painted gray while the new one is painted white. Of course new ones can be repainted gray. It is up to the buyer to judge whether it is a repainted bank, or whether what he sees is a natural accumulation of grime and dirt from handling. Plate 148.

REMADE BANKS

1. Cat Chases Mouse into Building bank. This was assembled from toy parts. A cat goes into a building and a mouse darts out. Picture shows remade bank. Plate 149.
2. Target bank. A man sitting in a vestibule throws a coin over his head into a target, which is in back of him. A made-up bank using old still-bank and other parts.
3. Elephant on Wheels with Movable Trunk. Originally a bell-ringer toy, it has been altered by filing a coin slot in the elephant's body. It would not operate if a coin were inserted because the coin would interfere with the mechanism that operates the trunk. Do not confuse with Jumbo Baby Elephant on Wheels.

RECAST BANKS

1. Standing Dog bank. Place a coin on tongue, push tail and the dog swallows the coin. Many recasts of this bank, which usually show rough and sharp edges. The old bank is smooth inside and out.

Note: A good way of telling old banks is to open them up and look inside. Most old banks are smooth inside, due to the method used in making them years ago.

2. Owl bank. The owl turns head when you press lever and knocks coin into bank. Picture shows original on left and recast on right. Note detail on original. The recast has a baked enamel finish, heavy and very poorly fitted. Plate 152.
3. Paddy and His Pig bank. The illustration shows an original bank. The recast is heavy, poorly painted and rough. Plate 148.
4. Boy and Bulldog bank. Illustration shows an original bank. The recast is difficult to distinguish as some original patterns of this bank exist; however, they are rough and not smooth like old banks. Plate 153.

5. Darky on Bucking Mule bank. Pictured is an original bank. The same difficulty applies to this one as in the case of the Boy and Bulldog bank. Plate 152.

6. Tabby bank. Picture of an original bank is shown here. The recast is heavy and rough. Surface sometimes pebbly. The original is cast iron, while some new ones appear to be made of bronze or brass. Plate 151.

7. Gem bank. Original shown. The recast is heavy and rough, and painted black. Plate 151.

8. Goat Butting Tree Stump bank. This bank is small and just as its title implies. Same conditions exist as in the Boy and Bulldog bank.

9. Bear with Slot in Chest.

10. Bear with Paws around Stump.

11. Tricky Pig bank—picture shows doubtful bank. Plate 154.

DOUBTFUL BANKS

1. Lost Dog bank.

2. Barrel with Movable Arms bank.

3. Surly Bear bank—recast of bear with slot in chest.

4. Bull or Steer with Movable Horns.

5. Elephant with name *Hannibal* inscribed on side.

6. Glutton bank—probably made from inkwell.

7. Squirrel bank—made in lead or iron. Name of squirrel on back. Very heavy and probably made from a nutcracker. Picture shows doubtful bank. Plate 154.

8. Feed the Kitty bank—picture shows doubtful bank. Plate 149.

9. Ferris Wheel bank—believed to be a doctored-up old toy Ferris wheel put on a cast-iron base. Probably made in Providence, Rhode Island. These are still being converted today, whenever one turns up.

10. Chinaman with Rat on Tray. This is said to have been made as a souvenir for a dinner, and was never intended as a bank.

11. Metropolitan bank. This is a converted still-bank, probably being made over in Providence, R. I.

MODERN PREWAR BANKS

The Hubley Manufacturing Company of Lancaster, Pennsylvania, until the last war (World War II) made three mechanical banks, as pictured: Trick Monkey bank, Trick Dog bank and Elephant with Howdah bank. They discontinued manufacturing these banks immediately after the start of the war and as yet are not planning to resume manufacturing. They now have some value in a collection but not when "antiqued" and made to look old and misrepresented.

Chapter XV

IRONWORK

It is not my intention to delve extensively into the subject of cast-iron reproductions, since the demand for the old itself is not very great. There are, however, excellent copies of old garden furniture which are worthy of mention, to say nothing of other interesting garden accessories.

Cast-iron andirons of good design have been reproduced for years, some of which I doubt whether an expert could tell from the old. Figures of Hessian soldiers and a figure of George Washington were favorites with the copyists because of the popular historical association.

Owners of country estates have long been interested in the old iron hitching posts in the forms of jockey boys, slave boys, etc., which sold at very good prices. New ones have been cast and sold during the past several years. Even the hitching posts surmounted by horses' heads are now made. One is shown on Plate 155. The safest procedure for a buyer who does not feel sure is to be guided by the conditions under which the piece is sold. If a dealer is willing to give a money-back guarantee, at least one objection is removed. Another method is to learn the circumstances attending the acquisition of the piece by the dealer, who, incidentally, should be above suspicion of mendacity. Sometimes one knows the family history, which obviates the need of further questions. If one pays the price of a new specimen sold frankly as such, there should be no comeback. Collectors who are forever seeking bargains run the risk of getting exactly what they pay for and no more.

Iron garden furniture, long a favorite, is being made in the South. On Plates 155 and 156 may be seen some of the patterns reproduced today. The grape as well as the fern leaf have been popular for many years.

Plate 155
IRON HITCHING POST AND GARDEN ACCESSORIES FROM VIRGINIA,

Plate 156

REPRODUCTIONS OF FAVORITE PATTERNS IN OLD IRON
GARDEN FURNITURE.

Plate 157
IRON URNS AND A GARDEN TABLE.

Plate 158

COPIES OF FOOT-SCRAPERS, EARLY LANTERNS AND OTHER IRONWARE.

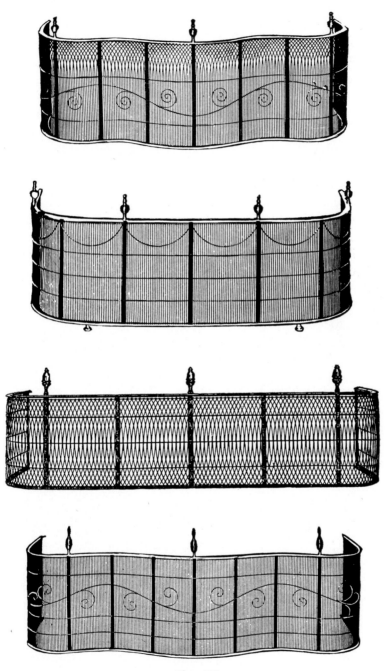

Plate 159
NEW FIREPLACE FENDERS.

Iron garden tables and flower urns, also made in the South, are seen on Plate 157. There is some demand for these, though it is not as great as for the furniture. Other small objects are copied, such as trivets, frog doorstops, foot scrapers, skillets, etc.

Lanterns have been reproduced for a long time, ever since the demand for new Colonial homes existed. They fit in so nicely, and save the trouble of hunting for old ones, and having them wired. Old lanterns are plentiful enough, though it often seems that any antique proves elusive when one wishes to find it in a hurry. Some of the above are illustrated on Plate 158.

Good old fenders often prove a source of worry to collectors. I presume it is the reason that so many buy the new ones. On Plate 159 are illustrated several patterns being made today. They are advertised as authentic reproductions, handmade and correct in every detail. The advertised prices of the copies are higher than I have often seen the genuine old ones sell for, probably because labor costs today are much higher.

Chapter XVI

NOVELTIES

It would scarcely be possible to enumerate, far less to illustrate, the infinitude of objects that sometimes find their way into antique shops, which properly belong to the gift shop trade. However, it is a well-established fact that certain glass concerns have thrived on a business devoted largely to outright copies of old pieces, or patterned after their style in a manner that deceives uninformed dealers and collectors. Moreover, many of such items are produced with the anticipation that they will find an active market with unscrupulous antique dealers. It is for this reason that some of the more prominent pieces will be illustrated and discussed here.

A collectible item which aroused more than passing interest during recent years has been glass baskets. They were produced chiefly during the 1870's and 1880's, and many of them are beautiful pieces of art work. They were made in Satin glass, as well as in various combinations of colored glass. The handles are fluted, often twisted at the top; others are more elaborate, with thornlike projections as shown in the one on Plate 160. The first reproduction I came across is the one at the left. It is a medium-sized basket, in a bizarre color combination, that is rather more striking than any I have seen in old ones, in black, yellow, red, etc. The top is fluted, and the evidence of newness is in the pontil on the base, which is ground out and left with a highly frosted finish. Most old baskets have a rough, scarred pontil. While some may be found with pontil ground out, they would not be left frosted. The bowl of the reproduction is further embellished with medallionlike ornaments, slightly raised and somewhat similar to a flattened hobnail. I have seen another reproduction in the same combination of colors and with the same style of crystal handle, without the ornamentation on the bowl.

I have never seen an old basket like the new one pictured. Next to the new basket is a typical old one. This has a plain bowl with fluted edge and simple, twisted crystal handle. The colors are a soft pink and opaque-white, in a "splashed" effect. Some of the most attractive of the old baskets are decorated with applied flowers or fruit, in various colors. Many such novelties were produced by Hobbs, Brocunier & Co., of Wheeling, West Virginia, and other factories in the old Pittsburgh glass district.

A number of new Satin glass baskets have appeared in recent years, also. There is a seven-inch (to top of handle) size, six and one-half inches in diameter, advertised in pink or blue "Overlay Satin." The same colors are utilized in a slightly smaller Satin basket, six and one-half inches high and four inches in diameter.

One glass company has made a number of baskets in "case glass," meaning two layers of glass. Some of these are milk-white on the inside, clear outside, with round bowls having a frilled edge. The handles are in milk-white. Others are in a combination of pink and clear case glass. The new extra large colored hobnail baskets are so obviously new that they should not deceive anyone. More attractive are the small rose diamond-quilted baskets. These were produced for department stores and gift shops.

Other new Satin glass objects include pink or blue barber bottles; pink or blue melon-shaped cruets and melon-shaped night lamps with ball globe. These are made in more than one size, in pink and in blue "Satin Overlay." There is one large size, measuring eight and one-half inches. A hand holding a cornucopia vase beaded about the center with a fluted top, is made in two sizes, nine and ten inches tall, in pink, and blue Satin glass. A new Satin glass vase is pictured on Plate 96, which came out in several variations during the 1930's. It does not compare favorably with the old ones. The genuine style, in case glass, has a thick white lining. The new are thin, with the handles usually frosted in the same color as the vase, which was never done originally. The base should be stamped MADE IN CZECHOSLOVAKIA, but those I have seen had this identification carefully ground out.

Hand vases, holding a cornucopia-shaped flower container, are made in five distinct types. One is illustrated on Plate 45 in the Daisy and Button pattern. Several are also pictured on Plate 66. A third style, not illustrated, with a fluted top, eight and one-half inches high, is made in milk-white, opaque-blue, and frosted. Another is smaller, and has a hand clasping a sheaf of wheat. These measure six inches tall and are made in amber, and perhaps other colors. The fifth type is the one described in the preceding paragraph, on Satin glass.

A considerable quantity of new cranberry glass has continued to flow into dealers' shops, often purchased by unsuspecting, honest proprietors. It is sufficient to say that all of it is too heavy, and sometimes the shade of color is off, as well.

There are a good many new cruets out, as might be expected since these are a popular collectible today. Among these are the cranberry Inverted Thumbprint, with a clear hexagonal stopper and clear reeded handle. This has three widely spaced rows of much too large thumbprints. The same type is made in blue, and it will be surprising if other colors do not appear. Cranberry and blue Spanish Lace cruets have been about for some time. The design is diffused through the glass in the new, instead of being clear and sharp, as may be noted in the tumbler illustration on Plate 71. The above-listed cruets, added to those mentioned among the Satin glass items, constitute quite an array but will not distress collectors or dealers, once they are on their guard. As this goes to press, new Burmese cruets have appeared, in a fluted pattern, complete with stopper.

New barber bottles follow a similar pattern. They may be found in what is known as the "Stars and Stripes" design. Like the new Spanish Lace, the pattern is not sharp enough. The two styles of Hobnail barber bottles are illustrated and discussed in the pattern glass chapter. Doubtless there are other new barber bottles which I have not seen or heard about.

There are so many novelty lamps on the market that the only way one may be certain about them is in the brass collars, or other fittings. There are numerous sizes and patterns in new "Gone with the Wind" lamps. There are also a number of sizes and styles in student lamps. While some of the reproductions are exceedingly poor, it must be said that many of the novelty lamps are extremely attractive. One type has a milk-white base, cranberry bowl and cranberry chimney. A milk-white nine-and-one-half-inch lamp carries the Cosmos pattern on the bowl. Another has a clear bowl with a copy of the old "Shields and Stars" design in the bowl. One advertised as Moon and Star is definitely not that pattern. The design consists of round thumbprints, alternating with five-pointed stars. Some of these are in odd combinations of colors, such as amber bowls with blue bases.

Many modern, attractive epergnes may be seen in the shops, styled after the old. I saw one in amethyst, having four branches which were edged in milk-white. This one was seventeen inches tall. Another was in opalescent, the design consisting of diamond-shaped spaces, each containing a hobnail. There are others in pastel shades, edged with contrasting colors.

Numerous novelty hats have been seen here and there, since the 1930's. The extra-large one shown on Plate 161 is not a known copy of any old example. It is found in fine shades of amethyst, sapphire blue, emerald green, amber, and clear glass. I have been told they could have been purchased from jobbers in New England, about fifteen years ago, at $6.00 each. In antique shops, I have seen them retail as high as $25.00! The tale reached me that these were made at one time, by the old Pairpoint Glass Company, at New Bedford, Mass.

A hat made in what was originally termed the "Diamond" pattern by Mr. Charles West, founder of the Westmoreland Glass Company, but known today as English Hobnail, may be seen on Plate 162. These came out in the late 1890's and early 1900's, in clear glass and in colors.

New Crackle glass hats have been about for some time. All authentic old ones had metal brims, so the modern offer no problem. The new specimens are match-holder size and the brim is plain, without any pattern.

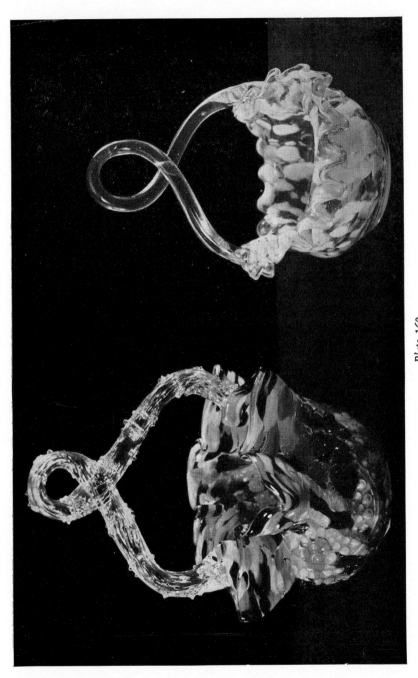

Plate 160

AN OLD AND NEW VICTORIAN BASKET. AN ORIGINAL IS AT THE RIGHT.

Plate 161

MODERN HAT, IN AN EXTRA-LARGE SIZE.

Plate 162

NEW ENGLISH HOBNAIL HAT. MODERN BUTTERFLY TODDY PLATE.

Plate 163

MODERN NOVELTIES.   THE BIRD SALT AT THE END IS OLD.

Plate 164

MODERN NOVELTIES. THE SECOND BIRD SALT FROM THE END IS OLD.

Plate 165
COPY OF AN EARLY SANDWICH VASE.

GIFT-SHOP MERCHANDISE, NOT TO BE CONFUSED WITH OLD PIECES.

Plate 166
PAPERWEIGHTS WHICH CAME OUT SOME YEARS AGO.

All sorts of new hats in swirls, inverted thumbprints, stripes, and in case glass (clear over pink, etc.) with frilled edges, from match-holder size up to seven-inch models, popular for popcorn at cocktail parties, may be seen in almost any gift shop. Corresponding old ones to most of these models, are unknown. Copies of earlier blown glass hats will be found in the chapter dealing with blown glass reproductions.

Among other novelties which were abroad during the 1930's is a frosted fish match holder, which is shown on Plate 163. These were never made in old glass, as far as I can learn, but have been finding their way into a few collections.

Copies of the blue bird salt, with a cherry in its beak, have been widely advertised. The flat type, shown on Plate 163, was never particularly popular, so there was not much point in reproducing it. The new bird is at the left, the old one being at the end of the line. Small bird salts with uplifted wings have had widespread appeal for some years. Copies of these came out in the 1930's in an exceptionally wide range of colors, including blue, yellow, amber, amethyst, etc. An old one is pictured on Plate 164 but it is so small that the detail does not show. The originals have eyes set in a better position and they are clearly defined by two circular depressions. In the new, the eyes are larger and not so well defined. By and large, these particular bird salts are good copies. The old were produced in a limited color range, including blue, amber, yellow and clear glass. The copies may be found in almost any color, such as amethyst, green, sapphire-blue, etc. The bird salt without a cherry in the beak has not been reproduced.

At the extreme left on Plate 164 is a curious bird salt, which more nearly resembles a toad. It is unlike any known old one.

The miniature turkey on Plate 164 is a copy of the large one, which was popular during the 1870's. They have been in circulation for about twenty-five years.

In the center of Plate 164 is a copper luster pitcher which is typical of many new ones which are American made. I have been informed that several girls who worked in France are now employed in this country painting the colored bands, which help to make the new goods more attractive. These jugs are produced in a number of sizes and all have the hand-painted decoration like the one shown in the illustration, as well as other similar designs. The new pitchers are heavier in weight than the old, and any collector of experience would detect the newness of the decoration. Many of these jugs have found their way into antique shops. The large-size pitchers wholesale at from $3.00 to $4.00 each and are seen priced at anywhere from $6.00 to $22.00.

The kitten in the boot, on Plate 164, is merely ornamental. I never saw an old one like it. They serve no useful purpose, since they cannot hold matches or be used as containers. The small slipper on roller skates next to it is just one more object for the novelty hunter to beware of—at the price of an original!

The blue marble vase on Plate 165 should not be in a chapter devoted to novelties but neither did it fit properly under any other chapter heading. Since several copies of this early Sandwich vase have been seen at antique shows, it is important to picture it here. The base is hexagonal and the bowl has six panels, each having three large round thumbprints. The edge carries six scallops, and the over-all height of the vase is nine and three-eighths inches. The fakes are characterized by unusual shades of color, and in addition are usually extremely heavy. A tale has reached me that these are being executed by an individual workman in New Jersey. The vase is made in more than one size. As this goes to press, copies of New England Peachblow are reported. These are thin, apparently blown in sets comprising such items as plates in two sizes, goblets, cups and saucers, wine jugs, sugar and creamers, etc.

The copy of the so-called Staffordshire vase on Plate 86, which has been so popular in summer cottages for flowers, was made in Portugal and is so stamped on the base. It is so shining and new looking that it would not deceive anyone, unless the stamp were removed and the vase then subjected to a clever aging process. They are made in several sizes. The one illustrated measures four and three-quarters inches.

As stated in the beginning, it would be impossible to enumerate, far less to illustrate, all the infinitude of objects that belong to the gift shop trade but sometimes find their way into antique shops. The studious collector is not apt to be deceived. The ignorant collector who merely follows fads is apt to forget there is no royal road to knowledge. There are no short cuts. If he does not choose to protect himself by knowing what he buys, then he is bound to have to learn the hard way. *Caveat emptor* is not an empty phrase!

INDEX

Adams, Pygan, 252.
Adams & Company, 148, 212.
Albany Glass Works, 63, 73.
Alphabet plate, 164.
Amelung glass, 49.
American Glass, George and Helen McKearin, 73.
American Glass Cup Plates, Ruth Webb Lee and James H. Rose, 75.
American paperweights, 202, 210; *Plates* 106, 110.
American pressed glass, early, 3, 4.
American silver, fakes, 244–252.
Andirons, iron:
 George Washington, 284.
 Hessian soldiers, 284.
Animal dishes, list of reproductions, 183, 184; *Plates* 94, 95, 97, 116.
Animals:
 Miniatures, 22; *Plate* 12.
 Staffordshire, 259; *Plates* 141, 142, 143, 144, 145, 146.
Ash trays:
 three-mold, 39.
 Daisy and Button, 117.
Avery, C. Louise, 244.

Baby's shoe, 165; *Plate* 67.
Baccarat, 153; *Plate* 91.
Baccarat paperweights, 188; *Plate* 98.
Bakewell, Peats & Company, 137.
Baltimore Pear:
 goblets, 138, 164; *Plate* 83.
 plates, 138, 164.
 sauce dishes, 138, 164.
 sugar bowls, 138.
Banks, iron, 269–283.
Barber, George, 190, 192.
Barber, Harry, 190, 192.
Barber, Ralph, 190, 192.
Barber bottles, 292, 293; *Plate* 62.
Barrel with Movable Arms bank, 282.
Baskets, glass, 291, 292; *Plate* 160.
Basketweave pattern, 164.
Beaded Grape, goblets, 137, 164; *Plate* 82.

Beakers:
 fake John Burt, 252; *Plates* 135, 136.
 fake Vanderburgh, 251; *Plate* 134.
 genuine Vanderburgh, 251; *Plate* 133.
Bear with Paws Around Stump bank, 282.
Bear with Slot in Chest bank, 282.
Beehive pattern, 153.
 on Lacy Sandwich cake plate, *Plate* 91.
Beer sets, 14.
Before and After Marriage cup plates, 80, 81, 82; *Plate* 41.
Bellflower water tumbler, 164.
Benjamin Franklin cup plates (*see* Franklin cup plates).
Berry pattern, 125, 253, 254; *Plate* 138.
Besly, Thauver, 252.
Bird salts, 302; *Plates* 163, 164.
Bitters bottles, 51.
Blackberry pattern, 125.
 creamers, 126, 164, 185.
 goblets, 126, 164, 185; *Plate* 71.
 milk-white pattern glass, 185; *Plate* 71.
Blackberry Variant, 164.
Block and Fan Variant, milk-white pattern glass, 186; *Plate* 94.
Blown glass, 7, 11–50.
 fakes, 12, 13, 14, 21, 32, 33.
 how to tell genuine, 12, 13, 14, 21, 32.
Blue bird salts, 302; *Plates* 163, 164.
Bohemian glass, 11, 227–236.
 appreciation of new and old, 227.
 cut glass, 227.
 decanters, 235; *Plate* 123.
 differences between old and new, 236.
 engraved ruby, 228, 235; *Plates* 122, 124, 125
 pinch-bottle cordial set, 228; *Plate* 123.
 ruby, 212, 227; *Plates* 123, 124, 126, 127.
 service plates, 235; *Plate* 125.
 tableware, *Plates* 125, 126.
 vases, 228; *Plate* 124.

Booz, E. C., 56.
Booz Log Cabin bottle (*see* E. C. Booz
   Old Cabin Whiskey bottle).
Boston and Sandwich Glass Company,
   153, 188, 237.
Bottles:
   barber, 292, 293.
   barrel-shaped, 64.
   bitters, 51.
   blown pattern-molded, 65–72.
   Booz Log Cabin, 14; *Plate 32.*
   Castor, 21.
   Cornucopia-Basket of Fruits, 52, 53,
      73; *Plate 29.*
   Czechoslovakian, 54, 65; *Plates 30,*
      34, 36.
   diamond-quilted, 21, 22, 64, 65, 66;
      Plates 7, 34.
   diamond-quilted Stiegel type, 22·
      frontispiece.
   fakes; *Plates* 15, 28, 29, 30, 31, 32, 33,
      34, 36.
   Fislerville Jenny Lind, 53, 54, 73;
      Plates 30, 31.
   freak, 64, 72.
   genuine Stiegel diamond-quilted, 65;
      Plate 35.
   Horse and Cart, 55, 63, 74; *Plate 28.*
   ink, 51.
   Lowell Railroad-eagle, 63; *Plate 32.*
   Lowell Railroad-Washington, 63;
      Plate 33.
   Madonna, or Virgin, 41.
   Mexican, *Plate 31.*
   miniatures, 22; *Plate 11.*
   Ohio Stiegel type, 21.
   paperweight, 192; *Plate 103.*
   modern South Jersey; *Plates 37, 38.*
   perfume, 192.
   pickle, 51, 52.
   Plantation Bitters, fake, 52; *Plate 28.*
   spring water, Moses type, 64.
   Sunburst pattern, 53, 73.
   test for, 32.
   three-mold, 72; *Plate 15.*
   Violin, 53, 73.
   Washington, 53, 56, 57, 63; *Plate 29.*
   Washington Calabash, 57; *Plate 30.*
   Washington-Taylor, 57, 63.
Bowls:
   amber, 11, 12; *Plate 3.*
   Bohemian, 228; *Plate 122.*

Bowls (*cont'd*)
   Czechoslovakian, 41.
   Daisy and Button, 167.
   finger, 149, 150, 152; *Plate 79.*
   Inverted Thumbprint, 151; *Plates 79,*
      87.
   Lily-pad, 23, 32, 33, 66; *Plate 14.*
   milk, 13, 14; *Plate 4.*
   reproductions; *Plates 3, 4.*
   sugar (*see* Sugar bowls).
   test for glass, 32.
Boy and Bull Dog bank, 281; *Plate 152.*
Bread plate, Lion pattern, 128.
Brevoort, John, 252.
Brigden, Zacariah, 252.
Bristol glass, 7.
Bull or Steer with Movable Arms bank,
   282.
Bull Dog Savings bank, iron, *Plate 153.*
Bunker Hill cup plates, 80, 81; *Plate 41.*
Burt, Benjamin, 252.
Burt, John, 252.
Butter chips, Daisy and Button, 165.
Butter dishes, 128, 136, 154.
Butterfly cup plate, 79, 80, 81; *Plate 40.*
Butterfly toddy plate, modern, 80;
   Plate 162.

Cake plates:
   Lacy Sandwich, 153.
   Sandwich octagonal Beehive, 153,
      154; *Plate 91.*
Candlesticks:
   Bohemian, 228; *Plate 124.*
   brass, 225.
   dolphin, 237–243.
   examples, *Plate 115.*
   "Petticoat" dolphin, 242, 243.
"Cane and Spray," 154, 155, 174;
   Plate 68.
Canes:
   how made, 189, 190; *Plate 100.*
   in paperweights, 188.
   pieces used in old paper weights, 189;
      Plate 100.
   sections used for decorative purposes,
      188
Carboys, 51
Carlsbad china, 253; *Plate 138.*
Carnival bank, 279, 280.
"Case" glass, 236; *Plate 147.*
   baskets, 292.

"Case" glass (*cont'd*)
  how made, 211.
Cat Chases Mouse into Building bank,
  iron, 279, 280; *Plate* 149.
Celery dips, Daisy, 150.
Celery vases, 97, 118, 127, 128, 170;
  Plate 73.
Ceramics, 253–268
Champagnes. *See* Wine glasses.
"Check List," Van Rensselaer, 51, 52.
Cherry goblet, 149, 164; *Plates* 54, 78.
Chinaman with Rat on Tray bank, 282.
Chinese paperweights, 200, 201; *Plates*
  105, 106.
Chicken on Basket (*see* Hen covered
  dishes).
Clearwater Collection, 244.
Clichy paperweights, 188.
Coffeepot, 251.
Colored glass curtain tie-backs, 163.
Compotes:
  Bohemian, 235; *Plate* 125.
  Crystal Wedding, 148; *Plate* 85.
  dolphin, 237–243.
  Lion pattern, 127, 128; *Plate* 72.
  Moon and Star, 172.
  Three face, 136.
  Westwood-Ho, 95.
Coney, John, 244, 252.
Console set, Bohemian, 228; *Plate* 122.
Consolidated Lamp and Glass Company,
  199.
Constantine, Emil, 199.
"Continuation glass," 125.
Co-operative Flint Glass Company, 125.
Copper lustre, 254, 302; *Plates* 139, 164.
Cordial glasses:
  Bohemian, 235; *Plate* 125.
  Ruby Thumbprint, 149.
Cordial sets:
  Bohemian, 235; *Plate* 127.
  Bohemian ruby, 235; *Plate* 127.
  pinch bottle, Bohemian, 228; *Plate*
  123
  price, 236.
Cornucopia-Basket of Fruit flask, 52,
  53, 73; *Plate* 29.
Cottage genre pottery pieces, 260.
Cotton stem glasses, 41.
Cowell, William, 252
Crackle glass hats, 294.
Cranberry glass, 293.

Crandall Manufacturing Company, 280.
Creamers, 14, 21, 33; *Plate* 5.
  Blackberry, 125, 126.
  copper lustre, 254; *Plate* 139.
  Hobnail, *Plate* 76.
  Inverted Thumbnail, 151.
  Ivy in Snow, 170.
  Lily-pad effect, 22.
  Lion pattern, 128.
  miniatures, 22; *Plate* 11.
  novelty, *Plate* 64.
  South Jersey reproductions, 21, 22;
    Plates 7, 9, 10, 11, 12.
  three-mold, 33, 39.
  Venetian and Bristol types, *Plate* 26.
"Crown weight," 189.
Cruets:
  Burmese, 293.
  Cranberry Inverted, 293.
  Hobnail, 106; *Plate* 61.
  Inverted Thumbprint, 151.
  Rose in Snow, 97.
  Spanish Lace, 152, 293.
  Thumbprint, 293.
Crystal Wedding:
  compotes, 148; *Plate* 85.
  goblets, 164.
Cup plates, 75–84.
  Before and after Marriage, 80, 81, 82;
    Plate 41.
  Bunker Hill, 80, 81; *Plate* 41.
  Butterfly, 79, 80, 81; *Plates* 40, 162.
  differences between old and new, 75.
  Eagle, 81.
  few fakes, 51.
  Franklin, 77, 78, 80; *Plate* 40.
  Henry Clay, 75, 76, 77, 80, 83;
    Plate 39.
  Historical, 82, 83; *Plates* 42, 43.
  modern commemorative, 82, 83; *Plates*
    19, 42, 43.
  reproductions, *Plates* 39, 40, 41.
  test for, 75.
  Thirteen Hearts, 80, 81.
  Valentine, 82; *Plate* 39.
  Washington, 83; *Plate* 43.
Cut glass, Bohemian, 227.
Curtain tie-backs:
  colored glass, 163.
  opal curtain, 163.
  pressed tin, 163.
  Sandwich opal, 163.

Curtain tie-backs (*cont'd*)
 silvered, 163.
 various types, *Plate* 93.
Czechoslovakian glass, 11, 53, 211, 236.
 "Stiegel," 40, 41.
 (*see also* Bohemian glass).

Daisy and Button:
 ash trays, 117.
 baby shoes, 165; *Plate* 67.
 butter chips, 165.
 bowls, 167.
 champagnes, 167; *Plate* 69.
 deep dessert dish; *Plate* 67.
 fakes; *Plate* 66.
 flat bow, 166.
 flasks, 165, 166.
 goblets, 117, 165, 167; *Plates* 54, 65,
  70.
 hats, 117, 118, 165.
 list of reproductions, 117, 165, 166,
  167.
 match holders, 118, 165.
 novelties, 118.
 plates, 117, 166; *Plates* 67, 68.
 Puss-in-boots, 166.
 slippers, 117, 166, 167; *Plate* 67.
 toilet sets, 167.
 trays, 167.
 vases, 117, 166, 167, 292, 293; *Plates*
  45, 66.
 wines, 167.
Daisy and Cube, 167; *Plate* 69.
Daisy pattern, 116.
 celery dips, 150.
 sauce dishes, 150.
Darky on bucking mule bank, 282;
  Plate 152.
Decanters:
 Bohemian, 235; *Plate* 123.
 diamond-quilted, 22, 23; *Plate* 13.
 modern, *Plate* 13.
 quart, 22, 23, 40; *Plate* 13.
Deer pattern lamp, 212; *Plate* 114.
Della Robbia, milk-white pattern glass,
  187; *Plate* 59.
Demijohns, 51, 64.
Dessert dishes, 14, 41; *Plate* 5.
Dew and Raindrop pattern, 167.
Diamond Cut with Leaf:
 goblets, 134, 167.
 wine, 134, 167.

Diamond pattern (*see* English Hobnail).
Diamond-patterned:
 flask, 65; *Plate* 36.
 sugar bowls, 22.
Diamond-quilted bottles, 21; *Plate* 7.
 Czechoslovakian fake, 65; *Plate* 34.
 genuine Stiegel, 65; *Plate* 35.
 goblets, 167.
 tumblers, 167.
Diamond-quilted Stiegel type bottles,
  23; *frontispiece.*
Diamond-quilted salts, 33; *Plate* 7.
Dishes:
 animal, 183, 184.
 butter, 128, 136, 154.
 dessert, 14, 41; *Plate* 5.
 hen covered, 183; *Plates* 94, 97.
 leaf sauce, 171.
 rabbit covered, 184.
 rooster covered, 183.
 swan covered, 184; *Plate* 97.
 sauce (*see* Sauce dishes).
Dixwell, John, 252.
Dog bank, iron, 281.
Dogs, Staffordshire, 260; *Plates* 142,
  143, 144, 145, 146.
Dolphin candlesticks, 237–243.
 double-step type, 238.
 how to tell genuine, 237, 238; *Plates*
  128, 129.
 modern, 242.
 old and new, 237, 238, 239; *Plates*
  128, 129.
 "petticoat," 242, 243.
 Pittsburg type, 240.
Dolphin compotes, 237–243.
 differences between old and new, 242,
  243; *Plates* 50, 130.
Donkey bank, iron, 279.
Door stops, 199; *Plate* 104.
 frog, 290.
 turtle, 11, 12; *Plate* 3.
Drake's Plantation Bitters bottles, 52.
Dresden:
 miniatures, 260.
 shoe, 260; *Plate* 147.
 toilet set, 260; *Plate* 147.
Duncan and Sons, George, 125.
Dutch beaker:
 fake Vanderburgh, 251; *Plate* 134.
 genuine Vanderburgh, 251; *Plate*
  133.

Dyottville, Washington-Taylor flasks, 64, 73.

Eagle—Cluster of Grapes, 63, 73.
Eagle—Cornucopia, 73.
Eagle cup plates, 81; *Plate* 41.
Early American Pressed Glass, Ruth Webb Lee, 6, 125, 138, 149, 150, 152, 164, 187, 212.
Early American Silver, Louise Avery, 244.
E. C. Booz Old Cabin Whiskey bottle, 14, 55, 56, 73; *Plate* 32.
  prices, 55, 56.
Edwards, John, 252.
Eggcups, 97, 128, 212; *Plate* 94.
Eggerman, design after, 228; *Plate* 124.
Elephant bank, iron, 282.
Elephant with Howdah bank, 283.
Elephant on Wheels with Movable Trunk bank, 281.
English beaker, fake John Burt, 252; *Plates* 135, 136.
English copper lustre, 254; *Plate* 139.
English Hobnail, milk-white pattern glass, 186; *Plate* 162.
English paperweights, 201; *Plate* 106.
Engraved glass, Bohemian, 228, 235; *Plates* 122, 124, 125.
Epergne, 294.

Faked American silver, 244–252.
Feed the Kitty bank, iron, 279, 282; *Plate* 149.
Fenders, fireplace, 290; *Plate* 159.
Fern pattern, iron, 284; *Plate* 156.
Ferris Wheel bank, 282.
Figurines, Staffordshire, 259; *Plates* 142, 143, 144.
"Fine Rib" goblet, 152; *Plate* 88.
Finger bowls, 14; *Plates* 5, 6.
  Bohemian, 235.
  Inverted Thumbprint, 150; *Plate* 79.
  Ruby Thumbprint, 149.
  Spanish Lace, 152.
Fireplace Fenders, 290; *Plate* 159.
"First in bed puts out the lights, the," 260.
Fislerville Glassworks, 55.
Fislerville Jenny Lind Calabash bottle: fakes, 53, 54, 73; *Plates* 30, 31.
  how to tell genuine, 54.

Flasks, historical, 51–74.
  few fakes, 51, 52, 63, 64, 65; *Plates* 28, 29, 30, 31, 32, 33, 36.
  list of reproductions, 73, 74.
  plaster of paris molds, 53, 63.
  pontil mark, 51, 64.
  prices, 53.
  Van Rensselaer's "Check List," 51, 52.
  (*see also* Bottles).
Flip glasses, 41.
Flower urns, iron, 290; *Plate* 157.
Foot-scrapers, iron, 290; *Plate* 158.
Forty-niner donkey bank, The, 279.
Franklin cup plates, 77, 78, 80; *Plate* 40.
Freak bottles, 64, 72; *Plate* 15.
Frog door-stops, iron, 290.
Frosted Circle goblet, 149, 168; *Plate* 84.
Frosted Coin toothpick holder, 138, 168.
Frosted fish match holder, 302; *Plate* 163.
Fruit, milk-white pattern glass, 187; *Plate* 59.
Furniture, garden, 284; *Plates* 155, 156, 157.

Garden accessories, iron, from Virginia, *Plate* 155.
Garden furniture, iron, 284; *Plates* 155, 156, 157.
Garden tables, iron, 290; *Plate* 157.
Garvan, Francis P., 252.
Garvan Collection, 251.
Garvin, Mabel Brady, 252.
Gem bank, The, 282; *Plate* 151.
German Wedgwood, 254.
Gift shop merchandise, *Plate* 166.
Gillinder and Sons, 88.
Girandoles, 224; *Plates* 118, 119.
Glass:
  list of reproductions, 164–176.
  ruby-red, 227.
Glasses:
  flip, 41.
  lemonade, 149.
  wine (*see* Wine glasses).
Globes, 211–226.
  hurricane, 225; *Plates* 113, 121.
Glutton bank, 282.
Goat Butting Tree Stump bank, 282.

Goblets:
  Baltimore Pear, 138, 164.
  Basketweave, 164.
  Beaded Grape, 137, 164; *Plate* 82.
  Blackberry, 126, 164.
  Bohemian, 235.
  Cherry, 149, 164; *Plate* 78.
  copy of early blown; *Plate* 70.
  Daisy and Button, 117, 165, 167;
    Plates 54, 65, 70.
  Fine Rib, 152; *Plate* 88.
  Frosted Circle, 149, 168; *Plate* 84.
  Herringbone, 138, 168.
  Hobnail, 104, 168; *Plates* 59, 65.
  Icicle, 169.
  Ivy in Snow, 118; *Plate* 55.
  Lace Dewdrop, 171; *Plate* 96.
  Lacy Sandwich, 171; *Plate* 65.
  Lion, 126, 127, 128, 171; *Plate* 75.
  Milk-white, *Plate* 71.
  Modern, 152; *Plate* 88.
  Moon and Star, 97, 172; *Plates* 53,
    54.
  New England Pineapple, 103, 172.
  New Lace Dewdrop; *Plate* 96.
  Opal fruit, 172.
  Paneled Grape, 135, 136, 172.
  Pleat and Panel, 135, 173; *Plate* 78.
  Red Block, 149, 173.
  Ribbon, 137, 173; *Plate* 81.
  Roman Rosette, 149, 173; *Plate* 84.
  Rose in Snow, 96, 173; *Plate* 51.
  Ruby Thumbprint, 149, 174; *Plate*
    86.
  Shell and Tassel, 134, 174; *Plate* 77.
  Strawberry and Currant, 138, 148,
    175; *Plate* 84.
  Thistle, 152.
  Thousand Eye, 128, 133, 134, 175;
    Plate 76.
  Three Face, 127, 136, 175; *Plate*
    80.
  three-mold, 39.
  Thumbprint, 150, 175; *Plate* 63.
  Waffle, 176.
  Westward-Ho, 88, 127, 176; *Plate*
    49.
  Wildflower, 87, 176; *Plate* 47.
Gold lustre, 254; *Plate* 138.
"Gone with the Winds" lamps, 224,
  294.
Grape pattern, iron, 284; *Plate* 156.

Grape pattern lamps, 212; *Plate* 114.
Grapevine pattern, Bohemian, 228.
Gypsy kettle, 117.

Hanging lamps, 225; *Plate* 120.
Hats:
  case glass, 302; *Plate* 63.
  crackle glass, 294.
  Daisy and Button, 117, 118.
  diamond pattern, 23.
  diamond-quilted, 21.
  English Hobnail, 163, 294; *Plate* 162.
  Inverted Thumbprint, 151, 302; *Plate*
    87.
  modern glass, *Plates* 8, 13.
  novelty, 294, 302; *Plates* 63, 161.
  plain blown glass, 14.
  price, 39.
  Sandwich, 40.
  three-mold, 33, 34, 39, 40; *Plate* 19.
  vertical rib, 21.
Hen covered dishes, 183; *Plates* 94, 97.
Henchman, Daniel, 252.
Henry Clay cup, 75, 76, 77, 80, 83;
  Plate 39.
Herringbone, green:
  berry bowls, 138.
  goblets, 138, 168.
  plates, 138.
  sauce dishes, 138.
Hessian soldiers, iron, 284.
Highball glass, Ruby Thumbprint, 149.
Historical cup plates, 82, 83; *Plates* 42,
  43.
Historical flasks, 51–74.
Hitching posts, iron, from Virginia,
  284; *Plate* 155.
Hobbs, Brocunier & Company, 292.
Hobnail:
  barber bottles, 104, 105; *Plates* 60, 61,
    62.
  creamers; *Plate* 76.
  cruets, 106; *Plate* 61.
  English, 163, 186; *Plate* 162.
  glass pump, 116, 117; *Plate* 64.
  goblets, 103, 104, 168, 172; *Plates* 59,
    65.
  jars, 103.
  modern examples, 116; *Plate* 63.
  opal, 104.
  perfume bottles, 103.
  pitchers, 103, 104, 169.

Hobnail (*cont'd*)
  reproductions, *Plates,* 58, 61.
  Rose-opalescent, *Plate* 60.
  salt, 106.
  sauce dishes, 103, 106; *Plate* 63.
  Shoes, *Plate* 76.
  Sugar bowls, 103.
  trough shaped dish, 116; *Plate* 64.
  types, *Plate* 57.
  vases, 103, 168. *Plates* 56, 57, 58.
  water tumblers, 104.
Horn of Plenty:
  how to tell genuine design, 8.
  lamp-bowl, 86.
  water tumblers, 8, 86, 169; *Plates* 44,
    45.
Horse and Cart bottle, 55, 73.
  fake, *Plate* 28.
Hourglass, 11, 12; *Plate* 3.
House pattern, pink lustre tea sets, 253;
  Plate 137.
Hubley Manufacturing Company, 283.
Hurd, Jacob, 252.
Hurricane globes, 225; *Plate* 113.

Icicle goblet, 169.
Ink bottles, 51.
Inkwell, Sandwich, 40.
Inverted Thumbprint:
  bowls, 150, 151; *Plates,* 79, 87.
  cranberry, 178; *Plate* 81.
  creamers, 151.
  cruets, 151, 293.
  finger bowls, 151.
  hats, 151; *Plate* 87.
  lamp bowls, 169, 212.
  lamps, 212.
  tumblers, 150, 151; *Plates* 79, 81.
  water pitchers, 151; *I lates* 81, 87.
Ironwork, 284–290.
Ivy in snow:
  butter dish, 170.
  celery vases, 118, 170.
  creamers, 170.
  goblets, 118; *Plate* 55.
  modern, 118.
  original molds, 118, 125.
  spoonholders, 170.
  sugar bowls, 170.

Jacobus, 88.
Jam jars, Turkey, 86, 175, 176.

Japanese Wedgwood, 254.
Jars:
  Bohemian, 128; *Plates* 122, 124.
  cathedral pickle, 64.
  hobnail, 103.
  jam, 86, 175, 176.
Jenny Lind calabash (*see* Fislerville
    Jenny Lind).
Jersey glass (*see* South Jersey).
Jockey boy hitching posts, iron, 284.
Jolly Nigger bank, iron, 280; *Plate* 148.
Jugs:
  Lily-pad, 32; *Plate* 14.
  Sunderland lustre Liverpool, 253;
    Plate 138.
  test for glass, 32.
Jumbo Baby Elephant on Wheels bank,
    281.

Kettle, Gypsy, 118.
King's Crown, 149, 169.
Kitten in the boot, 303; *Plate* 164.
Kitten milk-white plates, *Plate* 95.

Lace Dewdrop:
  butter dishes, 171.
  creamers, 171.
  goblets, 171; *Plate* 96.
  original molds, 125, 126.
  spoonholders, 171.
  sugar bowls, 171.
Lace Dewdrop, milk-white pattern glass,
    185, 186; *Plate* 96.
Lace-edged plates, 185.
Lacy pattern:
  copies of, 152, 153; *Plates* 65, 91.
  genuine Sandwich cake plate, 153;
    Plate 91.
  goblets, *Plate* 65.
"Lacy Sandwich" pattern, 152, 153, 171;
    Plates 65, 89, 91.
Lamp bowls, 8, 9, 211.
  Horn of Plenty, 86.
  Inverted Thumbprint, 212.
  overlay, 211.
  pear-shaped, 8, 9.
Lamps, 11, 12, 64, 211–226.
  Engraved Deer, 212; *Plate* 114.
  "Gone With the Winds," 294.
  Grape pattern, 212; *Plate* 114.
  hanging, 225; *Plate* 120.
  Hurricane, *Plate* 113.

Lamps *(cont'd)*
  Inverted Thumbprint, 212.
  Leaf pattern bowl, 212; *Plate* 115.
  modern, 212; *Plates* 114, 115.
  novelty, 212, 224, 293, 294.
  overlay, 8, 9, 211, 236; *Plates* 111,
    114, 115.
  peg, 211; *Plate* 111.
  reproductions, 9, 10, 212; *Plates,* 3,
    114.
  Sandwich heart pattern, 211; *Plate* 112.
  Sandwich style, 211, 224; *Plates* 112,
    113, 115, 117.
  Three face, 137.
  Westward-Ho, 95, 224; *Plates* 50,
    116.
Lamp shades (*see* Globes).
Lanterns, 290; *Plate* 158.
Lead-flint glass, 8.
Leaf sauce dish, 171.
Leigh, W. Colston, 191.
Lemonade glasses, 149.
Leverett, Knight, 252.
Lily-pad pattern, 22, 23; *Plate* 14.
  pitcher, 32, 33; *Plate* 15.
Lime glass, 8.
Lion pattern, 126, 127, 128, 171;
  Plates 72, 73, 74, 75.
Liqueur sets:
  Bohemian, 235; *Plate* 123.
  Bohemian ruby, 235; *Plate* 127.
Lizard paperweight, 202.
Long May it Wave bank, 279, 280.
Lord's Supper plates, 171.
Lost Dog bank, 282.
Lowell Railroad, 73.
  eagle bottle, 63; *Plate* 32.
  Washington bottle, 63; *Plate* 33.
Lusters, case-glass, 236.

Madonna bottle, 41.
Maple Leaf:
  goblets, 172.
  sauce dish, 150.
Marble Glass, 171; *Plate* 97.
Match holders, 118, 302; *Plate* 163.
Mechanical banks, iron, 269–283; *Plates*
    148, 149, 150, 151, 152, 153, 154.
  fakes 279, 280.
  recast, 279, 281.
  remade, 279, 281, 282.
  how to tell old, 270, 278, 281.

Medicine vials, 51.
Mercury glass (*see* Silvered glass).
Metropolitan bank, 282.
Mexican glass, 11, 55; *Plate* 31.
  inferiority of modern, 41.
  modern, *Plates* 22, 23, 24.
Milk bowls, glass, 13, 14; *Plate* 4.
Milk-white glass, 177–187.
  kitten plate, *Plate* 95.
  list of reproductions, 185–187.
  new, *Plate* 94.
  rabbit plate, *Plate* 95.
  swan covered dish, *Plate* 97.
  tests for, 177, 178.
Milk-White Pattern Glass, list of repro-
    ductions, 185–187; *Plates* 59, 71,
    94, 96.
Millefiori paperweights, 188, 189.
Millville Mushroom paperweights, 192;
    Plate 103.
Millville Rose pattern, 190, 191, 192;
    Plates 101, 102.
Miniatures:
  animals, 22; *Plate* 12.
  bottles, *Plate* 11.
  chair, 260.
  creamers, *Plate* 11.
  Dresden, 260.
  lamp, 212, 213.
  piano, 260.
  settee, 260.
  sprinkling pot, 260.
  tobies, *Plate* 141.
  turkey, 302; *Plate* 164.
Monkey bank, iron, 269, 270, 282,
    283.
Moon and Star:
  celery vase, 97, 103.
  compotes, 172.
  counterfeits, *Plate* 53.
  egg cup, 97, 103.
  goblets, 97, 103, 172; *Plates* 53, 54.
  lamps 212.
  sauce dish, 97, 103, 172.
  water pitcher, 103.
Moon and Star variant, 125.
Mugs, 14.
Mushroom paperweights (*see* Millville
    Mushroom paperweights).
Myers, Myer, 252.

Nailsea glass, 7.

New England glass, 7, 33.
New England Glass Company, 188.
New England Pear paperweight, 210.
New England Pineapple goblet, 103, 172.
New York State glass, 7.
New York State milk bowl, *Plate* 4.
Novelties, 291–304.
Noyes, John, 252.
Nut dish, three-mold, 39.

Old Fashion glass, Ruby Thumbprint, 149.
Old Silver of Europe and America, E. Alfred Jones, 244.
Onckelbag, Gerrit, 252.
Opal curtain tie-backs, 163, 172.
Opal fruit goblet, 172.
Overlay glass:
 Bohemian, 236.
 in colors, *Plate* 147.
 Czechoslovakian, 211, 236.
 domestic, 236.
 fakes of lamps, 8, 9.
 lamps, 8, 9, 211, 236; *Plates* 111, 114, 115.
 vase, *Plate* 119.
Overlay, "Spot Resist," 172.
Owl bank, 281; *Plate* 152.
O. W. plates, lace-edged plates, 185.

Paddy bank, iron, 270, 281; *Plate* 148.
Pairpont Glass Company, 41, 294.
Paneled Grape:
 goblets, 135, 136, 172, 173
 tumblers, 136; *Plate* 79.
Paneled Thistle:
 goblets, 135, 173; *Plate* 78.
 plates, 135, 173.
 salts, 135.
 champagnes, 173.
 wineglasses, 173.
Paperweights, 188–210.
 American, 202, 210; *Plates* 106, 110.
 bee pattern, 202.
 bird pattern, 202; *Plate* 110.
 bottles, 192; *Plate* 103
 Chinese, 200, 201; *Plates* 105, 106.
 English, 201; *Plate* 106.
 flower pattern, 189, 202; *Plates* 98, 99, 100.
 fruit pattern, 202, 210; *Plate* 109.

Paperweights (*cont'd*)
 hints for purchasing, 199, 200, 201, 210.
 history, 188, 189.
 how made, 189, 190, 199.
 interlaced background, 189; *Plate* 108.
 lizard pattern, 202.
 Millville Rose, 190; *Plates* 101, 102.
 modern, 202, 210; *Plates* 105, 107, 108, 109, 110.
 Mushroom, 192; *Plate* 103.
 new, 199; *Plates* 101, 102, 103, 104, 105, 107, 108, 109, 110, 166.
 old, *Plates* 98, 99, 101, 102, 103, 106.
 pig, 202, 210; *Plate* 110.
 pieces used in genuine old, *Plate* 100.
 snow-storm, 200.
 where made, 188.
Pattern glass, 3, 7, 85–176.
 fad for, 8, 51, 242.
Peg lamps, 211.
Perfume bottles, 192.
 paperweight, 192; *Plate* 103.
"Petticoat" dolphin candlesticks, 242, 243.
Phoenix Glass Company, 126.
Pickle bottles, 51, 52.
Pickle jars, 51, 52.
 Cathedral, 64.
 Milk-white pattern glass, 187; *Plate* 93.
Pig bank, iron, 282; *Plate* 154.
Pinch bottle cordial set, Bohemian, 228; *Plate* 123.
Pink lustre tea sets, House pattern, 253; *Plate* 137.
Pitchers:
 copper luster, 302, 303; *Plate* 164.
 Czechoslovakian, 4.
 fakes, 14; *Plate* 15.
 hobnail, 103, 104, 169.
 how to tell genuine, 33.
 Inverted Thumbprint, 151; *Plates* 81, 87.
 lily-pad, 32, 33; *Plate* 15.
 South Jersey reproductions, 14; *Plates* 1, 2, 5, 6, 7, 9, 10, 12.
 Spanish Lace, 152.
 three-mold 40; *Plate* 20.
 Westward-Ho, 96.
Plantation Bitters bottle, 52; *Plate* 28.

Plaster of Paris, 9, 53, 63.
Plates:
  Alphabet, 164.
  Beaded Grape, 137.
  Bohemian, 235.
  cake, 153; *Plate* 91.
  Cane and Spray, 155.
  Daisy and Button, 117, 118; *Plates* 67, 68.
  Ivy in Snow, 170.
  kitten milk-white; *Plate* 95.
  Lord's Supper, 171.
  Milk-white, list of reproductions, 184–185.
  modern, 152; *Plates* 31, 89, 90.
  open fan, 166.
  Paneled Thistle, 135.
  rabbit milk-white; *Plate* 95.
  Rose in Snow, 96; *Plate* 52.
  Sandwich octagonal Beehive Cake, 153; *Plate* 91.
  Spray and Cane, 154, 174; *Plate* 68.
  square, 88, 154, 166; *Plate* 68.
  Star with Dewdrops, 88, 174; *Plate* 46.
  Wildflower, 88; *Plate* 48.
Pleat and Panel goblets, 135, 173; *Plate* 78.
Pontil mark, 199.
Porcelain (*see* Ceramics).
Pottery (*see* Ceramics).
Presto Savings bank, iron, 280; *Plate* 150.
Puss-in-Boots slippers, Hobnail, 116.

Rabbit covered dishes, 184.
Rabbit milk-white plates, *Plate* 95.
Red Block, 149.
  goblets, 173.
  wines, 173.
Reproductions:
  items which may be mistaken for old, list of glass, 164–176.
"Return at one o'clock in the morning," 260.
Revere, Paul, 252.
Ribbon, goblets, 137, 173; *Plate* 81.
Richardson, Joseph, 252.
Ridout, George, 252.
Robin, animal dishes, 184; *Plate* 116.
Rod (*see* Cane).

Roman Rosette goblet, 149, 173; *Plate* 84.
Rooster covered dishes, 183.
Rose in Snow
  cruets, 97.
  goblets, 96, 173; *Plate* 51.
  plates, 96, 173; *Plate* 52.
Ruby-red glass, 227.
"Ruby Thistle" goblet, 152.
Ruby Thumbprint, 149, 170, 174; *Plate* 86.

Salad plates, Bohemian, 235.
Salts:
  bird, 302; *Plate* 164.
  blue bird, 302; *Plate* 163.
  Bohemian, 235.
  diamond-quilted, 33; *Plate* 7.
  footed three-mold, 33, 39, 40.
  Hobnail; *Plate* 63.
  Paneled Thistle, 135.
  Star with Dewdrop, 86, 87, 174.
  Swan, 187; *Plate* 146.
  swirled, 21.
Sanders beaker by Vanderburgh, 251.
Sandwich glass:
  hats, 40.
  heart pattern, 211; *Plate* 112.
  inkwells, 40.
  lamps, 211, 212, 224; *Plates* 112, 113, 115, 117.
  octagonal Beehive cake plate, 153; *Plate* 91.
  opal curtain tie-backs, 163.
  paperweights, 189.
  vases, 303; *Plate* 165.
Satin glass:
  baskets, 291, 292; *Plate* 160.
  barber bottles, 292.
  cruets, 292.
  vases, 292; *Plate* 96.
Sauce dishes:
  Daisy, 150.
  Herringbone, green, 138.
  Hobnail; *Plate* 63.
  leaf, 171.
  Lion, 127; *Plate* 74.
  Moon and Star, 97.
  Three Face, 136.
  three-mold, 33, 39.
  Westward-Ho, 95.
  Westward-Ho footed, 95.

Schwartz, Frank S., 190.
Service plates, Bohemian, 235; *Plate* 125.
Shell and Tassel, goblets, 134, 174; *Plate* 77.
Sherbets:
  Ruby Thumbprint, 149.
Shields, Thomas, 252.
Shoes:
  baby's; *Plate* 67.
  Dresden, 260; *Plate* 147.
  Hobnail; *Plate* 76.
  on roller skates, 118; *Plates* 76, 86.
Silver:
  considerations for buying, 244, 252.
  faked in America, 244–252.
  hints for detecting fake, 251, 252.
  marks, 251, 252.
  source, 244.
  style, 244.
  vetting, 244.
  workmanship, 246.
Silver lustre, 254.
Silvered or mercury glass, reproductions, 163, 174; *Plate* 92.
Silver resist, 253; *Plate* 138.
Silvered curtain tie-backs, 163.
Skillets, iron, 290.
Slave boy hitching posts, iron, 284.
Slippers:
  Daisy and Button, 117, 166, 167; *Plate* 67.
  Puss-in-Boots, 116.
  on roller skates, 303; *Plate* 164.
Snow-storm paperweights, 200.
Soumain, Simeon, 252.
South Jersey glass, 7, 11, 12, 13, 14, 21, 22, 23, 24, 32, 54, 63, 65, 66, 72, 73; *Plates frontispiece*, 1, 2, 3, 5, 6, 7, 8, 9, 10, 11, 12, 13, 14, 31, 32, 33, 36, 37, 38.
"South Jersey Stiegels," 41, 66.
Souvenir cup plates, 82, 83; *Plates* 19, 42, 43.
Spanish Lace, 151, 152, 174; *Plate* 71.
Spoonholders:
  Ivy in Snow, 170.
  Lace Dewdrop, 171.
  Lion, 127; *Plate* 62.
Spray and Cane (*see* Cane and Spray).
Spring water bottles, Moses type, 64.
Squirrel bank, iron, 282; *Plate* 154.
Squirrels, Staffordshire, 260; *Plate* 146.

Staffordshire:
  animals, 259, 260; *Plates* 141, 142, 143, 144, 145, 146.
  cottage ornaments, 260.
  figurines, 259; *Plates* 142, 143, 144.
  vases, 303; *Plate* 86.
Stag pattern, Bohemian, 228; *Plates* 122, 124.
Standing dog bank, 281.
Star with Dewdrop:
  baskets, 175.
  plates, 88, 174; *Plate* 46.
  salt, 86, 87, 174.
Stem glasses:
  Czechoslovakian, 41.
  Early English cotton, 41.
  New England cotton, 41; *Plate* 25.
Stiegel, Baron, 7.
Stiegel glass, 7.
  genuine diamond-quilted bottle, 65; *Plate* 35.
  imitations, 21, 23, 40, 41, 66.
  prices, 66.
Strawberry and Currant goblets, 138, 148, 175; *Plate* 84.
Sugar and Creamer, novelty, *Plate* 64.
Sugar bowls:
  diamond-patterned, 22.
  diamond-quilted, 22; *Plate* 11.
  fluted, 22.
  hobnail, 103.
  Ivy in Snow, 170.
  Lace Dewdrop, 171.
  open, lily-pad effect, 22; *Plates* 9, 10.
  three-mold, 33, 34, 39.
Sugar shakers, Spanish Lace, 152.
Sunburst pattern, 33, 39, 53, 74.
Sunderland Lustre Liverpool jug, 253; *Plate* 138.
Surly Bear bank, 282.
Swan, animal dishes, 184; *Plate* 97.
Swan salt, milk-white pattern glass, 187; *Plate* 146.
Syng, Philip, 252.
Syrup pitcher, Spanish Lace, 152.

Tabby banks, iron, 270, 282; *Plate* 151.
Tables, garden, 290; *Plate* 157.
Target bank, 281.
Tea sets, pink lustre, 253; *Plate* 137.
Teapots:
  fake John Coney, 244; *Plate* 131.

Teapots (*cont'd*)
  forgery of Coney's stamp, 244; *Plate* 132.
Ten Eyck, Koenradt, 252.
Thirteen Hearts cup plates, 80, 81; *Plate* 40.
Thousand Eye goblets, 128, 133, 134, 175; *Plate* 76.
Threading and superimposing glass, South Jersey technique of, 22.
Three Face pattern, 128.
  champagnes, 137.
  compotes, 136.
  goblets, 127, 136, 175; *Plate* 80.
  lamps, 137.
  sauce dishes, 136.
Three-mold glass, 33, 34, 39, 40, 73; *Plates* 15, 16, 17, 18, 19, 20.
  early fakes, *Plates* 15, 16.
  how to tell genuine, 39, 40.
  prices, 34, 39.
Three Panel goblets, 175.
Thumbprint pattern:
  goblets, 150, 175.
  imitations, 150; *Plate* 63.
Tiffany Favrile ware, 21.
Tin, pressed, curtain tie-backs, 163.
Tobies, miniature; *Plate* 141.
Toddy plate, Butterfly; *Plate* 162.
Toilet sets, Dresden, 260; *Plate* 147.
Toothpick holder, Frosted Corn, 138, 168.
Trays, Hobnail fanshaped, 116.
Trick dog bank, iron, 280, 283; *Plate* 151.
Trick elephant bank, iron, 280; *Plate* 148.
Trick monkey bank, iron, 269, 270, 282, 283.
Trick pig bank, iron, 282; *Plate* 154.
Trivets, 290.
Tulip, wines, 137; *Plates* 82, 175, 176.
Tumblers:
  Inverted Thumbprint, 150; *Plate* 79.
  Paneled grape, 136; *Plate* 79.
  Ruby Thumbprint, 149.
  Spanish lace, 151, 152; *Plate* 71.
  water (*see* Water tumblers).
Turkey, miniature, 302; *Plate* 164.
Turkey jam jar, 86, 175, 176.
Tyler, Andrew, 252.

United States Glass Company, 148.
Urns, flower, 290; *Plate* 157.

Valentine cup plate, 82; *Plate* 39.
Van der Spiegel, Jacobus, 252.
Van Rensselaer's "Check List" of historical flasks, 51, 52.
Vanderburgh, Cornelius, 251.
Vanderburgh beaker, 251; *Plates* 133, 134.
Vases, 14; *Plate* 6.
  Bohemian, 228.
  Bohemian, with design after "Eggermann," 228; *Plate* 124.
  celery, 97, 118, 127, 128, 170; *Plate* 73.
  Cornucopia, 292, 293; *Plates* 45, 66.
  Czechoslovakian, 41.
  Daisy and Button, 117; *Plates* 45, 66.
  diamond-pattern, 23.
  hand, 292, 293; *Plates* 45, 66.
  hobnail, 103, 168; *Plates* 56, 57, 58.
  overlay; *Plate* 119.
  paneled, 117.
  Sandwich, 303; *Plate* 165.
  Satin glass, 292; *Plate* 96.
  Staffordshire, 303; ***Plate* 86.**
  three-mold, 40; *Plate* 20.
Venetian type blown glass creamers, *Plate* 26.
Victorian baskets, *Plate* 160.
Vintage pattern, Bohemian, 228.
Violin bottles, 53, **74.**
Virgin bottle (*see* Madonna bottle).

Waffle goblet, 176.
Wall sconces, 10, 211; *Plate* 111.
Washington, George, iron, 284.
Washington:
  bottle, 53, 56, 63, 73; *Plates* 29, 33.
  calabash, 73; *Plate* 30.
  cup plate, 83; *Plate* 43.
Washington-Taylor flasks, **57, 63, 64,** 73.
Water pitchers (*see* Pitchers).
Water tumblers:
  hobnail, 104.
  Horn of Plenty, 86; *Plates* 44, 45.
  Inverted Thumbprint, 150, 178; *Plates* 79, 81.
  overlay; *Plate* 45.
  three-mold, 39.
  Three Paneled Grape; *Plate* 79.

"Wedding Night, The," 260.
Wedgwood and Sons, Josiah, 254.
Wedgwood:
  genuine, 254.
  German, 254.
  how made, 254.
  Japanese, 254.
  porcelain imitations, 259; *Plate* 140.
Wedgwood style porcelain, imitations, 259; *Plate* 140.
West, Mrs. Charles, 294.
Westmoreland Glass Company, 78, 79. 294.
Westward-Ho:
  compotes, 95, 176.
  footed sauce dishes, 95, 176.
  goblets, 88, 95, 127, 176; *Plate* 49.
  lamps, 95, 224; *Plates* 50, 116.
  pitchers, 96, 176.
  sauce dish, 95.
  wines, 95, 176.
White, Harry Hall, 55.
Whitney Glass Works, 55.
Wildflower pattern:
  goblets, 87, 88, 176; *Plate* 47.
  new plate, 178.

Wildflower pattern (*cont'd*)
  square plates, 88, 176; *Plate* 48.
Wine glasses, 11, 12; *Plate* 3.
  Bohemian, 235; *Plate* 123.
  champagnes, 149, 167, 173; *Plate* 69.
  Czechoslovakian, 41.
  Daisy and Button, 167; *Plate* 69.
  New England Pineapple, 103; *Plate* 55.
  Red Block, 149.
  Ruby Thumbprint, 149.
  Three face, 137.
  three-mold, 39.
  Thumbprint, 150.
  Tulip, 137, 175; *Plate* 82.
  Westward-Ho, 95, 176.
Wine sets:
  Bohemian, 235; *Plate* 123.
  Bohemian ruby, 235.
Wistarburg glass, 7.
Witch balls, 14.
Woodcock, Bancroft, 252.
Wynkoop, Benjamin, 252.

Yale University, 252.